AUSTRALIA

A Handbook for Living and
Working Down Under

FIACHRA Ó MARCAIGH
JESSICA CLASSON

THE MERCIER PRESS
CORK and DUBLIN

The Mercier Press Limited
4 Bridge Street, Cork
24 Lower Abbey Street, Dublin 1

© Fiachra Ó Marcaigh & Jessica Classon, 1988

ISBN 0 85342 835 2

For Deborah, Mark, Kate and Bob,
our friends in Australia.

Acknowledgements

The authors wish to thank the following for their help: the
staff of the Australian Embassy, Dublin; GL Robins, Mary
Woods, Caoimhín; DLS Travel, Dublin; Jane Agnew; Carmel
Burdett; Jacqueline Keane; Mike Murphy; Seumas Phelan;
Karen Heatley; Lesley Osborne; Siobhán Phillips; Sharon
Quigley; Frances Ní Fhlannchada; and Mark, for putting up
with us.

Printed by Litho Press Co., Midleton, Co. Cork.

Contents

Introduction

Well folks – this is it. The definitive guide to Australia for the Irish traveller, tourist or emigrant. And it's all in here – how to get there and what to do when you arrive. It's mainly for young people, but for any middle-aged adventurer who is contemplating a mid-life change – well you are in here too.

Australia is, these days, the 'in-place' and by the time 1988 has drawn to a close, we'll all be either heartily sick of hearing and reading about the place or we'll be packing our bags to go there. When we commenced our television adventure, two years ago, to make 'Murphy's Australia' we were obliged to draw on literally hundreds of sources of information for preliminary research. Had this book been around then we could have cut our workload in half.

These two young people compiled the enclosed in just over a year. How they did it I'll never know. They mustn't have had a moment to 'sink a tinnie' or 'throw a shrimpie on the barbie.'

But it is without question a *must* for any Irish person who has given even a passing thought to visiting or emigrating to the 'Lucky Country'.

Mike Murphy

The size of Ireland (bird) in relation to Australia

1 What's all this about Australia?

You are thinking about, or have decided on, trying Australia for a while, perhaps for a life time. Maybe you just want to visit and see what all the fuss is about. Despite the huge Irish interest in Australia at the moment, solid, up-to-date information is hard to come by.

You want detailed, factual information and advice on how to get there, find a job, find a place to live and get some idea of life in this society. There are plenty of guide-books suitable for tourists, but hard facts on the nuts and bolts of getting set up are scarce. We hope this book will fill this need, from visas to vehicles, and help you on your way.

Australia is a marvellous country, with many more opportunities than exist in Ireland at the moment, but they do not come easily. Australia has an unemployment problem too and there are many migrants, as well as Australians, competing for a place in the sun. Life is harder than it has to be if you do not start off with the right attitude, skills and information. We had a great time during our year there, but a book like this would have helped.

The decision whether to go or not is up to you. This book will let you weigh up the pros and cons and put you on the way to getting the most out of the Lucky Country. As they say down under, 'Go for your life!'

2 Getting In – Visas

Anyone who is neither an Australian citizen nor a New Zealand passport holder must have a visa to enter Australia. Naturally, the type of visa you look for will depend on what you intend doing in Australia. As with all visa applications, do not buy your ticket, quit your job or go around settling old scores until you actually have your visa.

All enquiries and visa applications should go to The Australian Embassy, Fitzwilton House, Wilton Terrace, Dublin 2. Telephone: 761517. The embassy is very busy these days and deals with these matters only from 8.30 to 12.30 on Monday, Tuesday, Thursday and Friday.

Visitor's visas are issued to people who are going to Australia for a short while – usually less than six months. The people normally covered by these visas are tourists, those visiting relatives, going on business trips or getting medical treatment.

To get a visitor's visa, you should fill out 'The Application to visit Australia' (form M48), which is available from the Embassy, and return it with a passport photograph. And don't forget your shovel. . . you must have a passport that will remain valid for the period of your stay.

People on visitor's visas are not allowed to work, to take up a course of study or to settle down. They are expected to go quietly at the end of their permitted stay. The Australians, naturally, take a dim view of people who try to stay on. If you do not abide by the conditions you may be denied a visa in future. Illegals are often caught and deported.

Working-holidays

These are issued under the Working-Holiday Scheme in an effort to foster cultural exchange between Ireland and Australia. Only single people or childless married couples are considered for this visa. The usual age limits are between 18 and 25 years, but there is a provision for making exceptions for people between 26 and 30 years of age if they can make a case for themselves.

It is not intended that working-holiday visa holders should immediately put their heads down and slave away in one place for the year. Keeping one job for more than three months is contrary to the spirit of the scheme. While the popular wisdom (rather than proven fact) holds that the tax office does not pass on information of this sort to the immigration authorities, it is still an abuse of the scheme to stick in one job. Thousands of Irish people have had a great time on one of these visas and Australia is generous in the number of them it provides for Ireland. It would be a shame if the scheme was cut back because of people from Ireland abusing it.

The prime objective is cultural exchange and those who are given visas are expected to have an interest in Australia and to be open-minded enough to profit from their experiences.

The conditions are not difficult to comply with. Among them are: that the applicant is visiting Australia for a specified period and does not intend to settle there; that working in Australia will only be an incidental part of the holiday and will only be to supplement holiday funds.

The applicant must not arrange work in advance except on a private basis and at his or her own initiative – this means that you write letters and that employment agencies are out until you get there. That much said, you must have 'reasonable prospects' of getting temporary work. This should not be too much of a problem, particularly if you are fit, keen and have skills and experience. A couple of contacts down under help too.

You must also have 'adequate funds', 'under the applicant's personal control' to pay for the holiday. That means that the money is shown on your bank statement. It does not allow for money that is tied up in assets or fond letters from home offering to sell the pig if you phone from Australia.

At the moment, 'adequate funds' means about £3,000 for a stay of one year. This would include the price of your return ticket.

Australia has had enough of what the gardaí call 'the criminal element' exported from Ireland and the British Isles. Therefore, 'applicants must meet normal character requirements and health standards where necessary.'

Maximum stay

The maximum stay allowed under the working-holiday scheme is 12 months. In some cases, the initial visa will be given for only six months. This seems to happen to people who apply at Australian Embassies overseas quite often. There is usually little problem about extending these visas to the full year once in Australia, provided the conditions of the visa have been kept and the applicant can show that there is enough left in the kitty for another six months. There is one problem in that the basic qualification for Medicare health insurance is that you have a visa that allows you stay in Australia for over six months. The Medicare office will not take it on trust that your visa will be extended, but you may approach the immigration authorities for an extension early in your stay. If this option fails, you will have to wait until you get your extension (usually about one month before the end of your visa period) before getting Medicare cover.

One extra problem with the initial six-month stay offered on some working-holiday visas is that it costs $50 to apply to get the visa extended. When this is added to the Medicare problem, you may think it worth your while to appeal to the embassy and offer to increase the amount of money you bring, or offer fuller proof of your intention to return to Ireland.

Temporary Residence

This is available to other people besides those on working holidays. They include the following:

Those taking up temporary work opportunities,
Academics taking up appointments,
Sportspeople,
Entertainers,
Those carrying out religious duties.

Generally, to be eligible for temporary residence, you must be sponsored by an employer or organisation in Australia. This sponsor must arrange suitable accommodation, ensure that you do not engage in activities other than those for which you were permitted to enter, ensure that laws relating to your employment are observed and be responsible for your departure, among other things. An accompanying spouse or children of working age would not be allowed to work. You may be subject to health and character checks before the application is granted.

Migration

Emigration to Australia is a whole new kettle of possums. Far more people want to go there than there is provision for. The tide is channelled through a number of categories in order to select those the Australian Government want to have and those who are best equipped for life in Australia.

When you first enquire, the Embassy will send you some leaflets. These cover the categories of immigration, the requirements and an outline of your chances. It is vital to read all this information carefully before applying. Leaving out details, failing to answer questions or not fulfilling the conditions will delay your application and exasperate those dealing with it. You probably need Australia far more than Australia needs you.

The basic immigration categories are; Family Migration, Skilled Labour Migration, Independent and Concessional Migration, the Employer Nomination Scheme and Business Migration Programme. Each will be dealt with in some detail.

There are a number of other categories, most of which are of less interest to young Irish people. They include: Retirement, for people over 55 who have substantial funds for transfer to provide for their retirement in Australia: Former Australian citizens who have maintained links with Australia but have lost their Australian citizenship: People with a record of achievement in creative or sporting activity which could benefit Australia: People of special ability who have distinguished themselves and who represent a clear gain to Australia: Refugees, displaced persons and those seeking entry to Australia on humanitarian grounds.

Family Migration

Family Migration generally applies to spouses, dependent children, parents and fiancés of an Australian citizen or a permanent resident of Australia (someone who has been accepted as a migrant to Australia). More distant relatives have to complete the points test, where they may get concessionary points for having an Australian relative who sponsors them. The sponsoring relative must be at least 18 years old. An extra condition, for those who are a parent, brother, sister, nephew, niece or adult child of the sponsoring relative, is that the sponsor must have been a legal resident of Australia for at least two years.

Sponsor's duties

Sponsorship by a close relative is one of the easier ways to get permission to settle in Australia, but it does make certain demands of the relative involved. Basically, the sponsor removes many of the risks being run by Australia in taking in a new person. Therefore, the sponsor is expected to give you information and advice to help you settle in Australia; to ensure that you have a place to stay; to provide financial assistance for your living needs in your first year in Australia. There are some other conditions too. If you are of working age and the parent, adult child, brother, sister, nephew or niece of your sponsor, the sponsor may possibly be asked to arrange a job for you. If you are the mother or father of your sponsor and aged over 50 (mother) or 55 (father) your sponsor must undertake to support you and to repay any benefits you get from the Government or from charities in Australia during your first ten years there, or up until the time you become an Australian citizen.

The sponsor should obtain the form 'Sponsorship for Immigration to Australia' from an office of the Department of Immigration, Local Government and Ethnic Affairs in Australia, complete it and send it to you. You should then lodge it with the Embassy in Dublin, together with your completed Immigration Application (form M47) and all the supporting documentation. The sponsor must include originals or certified copies of documents proving the relationship between you, and the sponsor's Australian citizenship, if the sponsor is an Australian citizen.

As well as the documents requested on the application form relating to your particular case, you must enclose copies of:
- full birth certificate for each person applying,
- civil marriage certificate, if applicable,
- death certificate of spouse or child if applicable,
- adoption, divorce, separation or custody documents.

The Dublin office then checks the sponsorship and application forms. If they indicate that you do not meet the requirements, you will get an explanation for the refusal and you will be told of your relative's right to appeal against the decision.

It is after this preliminary stage that the Embassy sometimes decides it is necessary for you to have work arranged by your sponsor. If this is the case you will be given a Confirmation of Offer of Employment (form M61), to send to your sponsor. If you pass this stage you may be called in for an interview at the Embassy, to assess your suitability and set the requirements. These requirements may include counselling sessions for migrants. You may fail at this point and, if so, you will be given the reasons and informed of your sponsor's right to seek a review of the decision. If you pass, you will be invited for a medical examination and the Australian authorities may be asked to check on your sponsor's capacity to provide for you in the future. The process may be delayed by incomplete forms, obtaining and checking an offer of employment, or by checks on character and health.

Independent and Concessional Migration
This is for people who are brothers, sisters, non-dependent children, nephews and nieces of the sponsoring relative and also others without a sponsor. Those with a sponsor should have a sponsorship form completed for them as for Family Migration, do a points test of themselves and if they score 70 points, lodge all the documentation with form M47 at the Embassy. To those without a sponsor, the authorities point out: 'Unless you have professional, technical or trade skills which can be fully recognised in Australia and several years' experience, you will not be able to accumulate sufficient points.'

You are told to consult the designated occupations list for details of training and experience requirements, although your occupation does not have to be on the list. The requirements are basically as follows – for tradesmen: AnCO Certificate of completion plus Department of Education or City & Guilds certificates plus several years' experience; for technicians and professionals: qualifications recognised in Australia plus three to five years' experience.

You should then make a points test and, if you hit the magic

70, lodge form M47 with the Embassy.

Remember
As well as the documents requested on the application form relating to your particular case, you must enclose copies of:
  − full birth certificate for each person applying,
  − civil marriage certificate, if applicable,
  − death certificate of spouse or child if applicable,
  − adoption, divorce, separation or custody documents.

The points test
The authorities say that 'mature young people who are educated, skilled and readily employable are most likely to meet the points assessment.'

The test applies only to the Independent and Concessional category of migration. The 'concession' is the extra points given for sponsorship by a relative who is not close enough to qualify you for family migration − parent, brother, sister, uncle or aunt. You gain ten points if you are brother, sister or the non-dependent child of the sponsor, five points if you are nephew or niece. Both categories gain an extra five points if the sponsor is an Australian citizen (as opposed to a permanent resident). The remainder of the points must be built up on the same points test as independent applicants (those with no sponsor). Remember that the sponsoring relative must have been legally resident in Australia for at least two years.

Employability
Immediately employable in a highly skilled, professional or technical occupation designated by the Department of Employment and Industrial relations as having good prospects (see list after this section) − 25.
Sound and continuous employment experience and needing no training − 20.
As above, but requiring limited training − 15.
Limited employment experience, but needing no training − 15.
Employment arranged by sponsor (on form M61) − 15
Limited experience, but requiring only limited training − 5.
Sound and continuous experience, but requiring extensive training − 5.
Limited employment experience and requiring extensive training − 0.

Skills (based on the occupation you are qualified for and intend to follow in Australia)
Recognised professional, technical or trade skills – 20
Professional, technical or trade skills not recognised – 10.
Clerical, administrative and semi-skilled – 10.
Unskilled – 0.

Education
Completed third-level, that is a course at university or college of advanced education leading to a bachelor's degree or higher – 20.
Full secondary, to matriculation level (12 years' schooling) or at least first part secondary then a course leading to a technical diploma or certificate, or a recognised trade – 15.
First part secondary, at least eight years' schooling – 10.
Less than eight years' schooling – 0.
These categories are set from the Australian system, in which eight years' education corresponds approximately to Inter Cert.

Age (at the time of assessment)
20-34 years – 15.
Under 20, or 35-44 – 10.
45 and older – 0.

Naturally, you can score only once in each category. If you are married, the partner who scores best should be regarded as the principal applicant. If you do not qualify at present, do not give up. While it is not possible to go back and re-arrange your family tree, you can certainly gain extra employability points by taking courses and getting experience.

Designated Occupations (to score 25 for Employability)

‡ Accountant
* Actuary
Binder and Finisher
Boilermaker
Bricklayer
Cabinet Maker
Carpenter (fixing and roofing)
Chef (Asian, French or other continental cuisine)

* Industrial Engineer
Metal Machinist (skilled)
Motor Vehicle Mechanic
Nurse
* Occupational Therapist
Offset Printer
Panel Beater
Pastry Cook
* Physiotherapist
Plumber

Compositor
* Computer programmer or
Systems Analyst
* Economist
Electrical Fitter/
Mechanic (Electrician)
* Electronic Engineer
Fitter
Fitter and Turner
Flexographic/Gravure
printer
Floor/Wall Tiler
Furniture Polisher
Graphic Reproduction
Printer
Hairdresser

* Quantity Surveyor
Radio and TV Repairer
Radiographer – Diagnostic
Sheetmetal Worker – skilled
* Speech Pathologist
Stenographer/Secretary,
60 wpm typing,
100 wpm shorthand
Stonemason
Sub-Editor/Journalist
Toolmaker/Diemaker
Turner
Upholsterer
Vehicle Painter
Waiter, skilled
Wood Machinist

* University degree or appropriate college diploma required
‡ ICAI

This list changes from time to time. Your occupation may appear in future, or if on it, may disappear. This is the list issued for the current financial year, (1 July 1987 to 30 June 1988).

Applicants who achieve 70 points are subject to the same interview, health checks, character checks and procedures as those outlined under Family Migration.

Skilled Labour and Business Migration

This includes three main categories: the Occupational Shares System, the Employer Nomination Scheme and the Business Migration Programme. All are aimed at making good shortages in the Australian labour market or taking in people who will be of benefit to Australia.

The Employer Nomination Scheme (ENS)

This allows employers to recruit highly skilled workers from overseas if they cannot fill their requirements from the local labour market or through staff training programmes.

The employer goes through the nomination process and the nomination is checked by the Department of Immigration, Local Government and Ethnic Affairs. It is then sent to the

Embassy in Dublin and you are invited to apply for migration to Australia. Your application involves verification of your qualifications to see that they match those described by the employer and the usual checks on health and character.

The nomination must meet the following requirements:

★ The job offer must be genuine, not just intended to help someone emigrate.

★ The vacancy must be for full-time, permanent employment.

★ The position must be highly skilled.

★ The terms and conditions of employment must not be less than the current market levels in Australia.

★ The employer must have a 'satisfactory training record'.

★ The employer must have tested the labour market by advertising the job widely and must be able to defend the decision to seek someone to fill it from overseas.

If you are nominated under ENS, you and your dependents must intend to settle permanently in Australia.

You must be under 55 years of age. The guides to occupations that are in demand under the Occupation Shares System and Independent and Concessional Migration may serve as some indication of jobs for which an employer might be allowed to sponsor you. If you are expert in a very specific field, you may also be in line for the ENS. Naturally, large companies are more likely to be able to spare the staff and to be doing the long-term planning involved in ENS recruitment.

Occupational Shares System (OSS)
The OSS is part of the planning process for the Australian economy which identifies shortages of people with particular skills and creates an opportunity for them to migrate to Australia. To qualify for this system, you must be under 45 years of age, have skills listed on the OSS list, have your qualifications recognised, be allocated a share and then pass other migration requirements such as health, character and settlement prospects. Like the longer list of designated occupations for the Independent and Concessional migration points test, the OSS list changes regularly.

Occupational Share System List for Skilled Labour Migration

‡ Accountant
Cabinet Maker
Chef – Asian, French or
other Continental Cuisine
* Computer Programmer/
Systems Analyst
* Economist
Electrical Fitter
Electrical Mechanic
Electronic Engineer
Furniture Polisher
* Industrial Engineer
Motor Vehicle Mechanic
Motor Vehicle Painter

Nurse
* Occupational Therapist
Panel Beater
Pastry Cook
* Physiotherapist
Plumber
* Quantity Surveyor
* Radiographer (diagnostic)
* Speech Pathologist
Toolmaker/Diemaker
Upholsterer
Waiter (skilled)
Wood Machinist

* University degree of appropriate college diploma required.
‡ICAI

This was the list for the 1986/87 year. The Embassy will supply you with the latest list.

If you satisfy the requirements for migration under the Occupational Shares System, complete form M47 and lodge it at the Embassy. You should have documentary proof of all your claimed skills and experience.

Business Migration

The Business Migration Programme is part of Australia's search for people with business expertise, capital and experience who can contribute to its development. More specifically, people are wanted who can:
  – Help reduce imports,
  – Increase the volume of exports,
  – Add value to exports,
  – Create skilled job opportunities,
  – Advance technological innovation.

You may be considered in two categories, depending on the amount of capital you possess. The first is for people with substantial capital and business experience and a good knowledge of business conditions in Australia. If going into a capital-intensive area of business, you would be expected to have minimum capital of $500,000. The second category includes people who do not have as much capital or business experience, but are judged to have the skills to establish a successful business in Australia. Generally, they are expected to have capital of at least $150,000.

If you feel you are eligible, make an appointment with the BMP officer at the Embassy, who will set out the programme in detail for you. All Australian States are anxious to have successful businesses located in them. The Embassy will give you more information about the programme and a list of Australian offices that will be happy to help you.

Student Entry

There are provisions for people to enter Australia to study. The Embassy can supply detailed information, but the general requirements for you to be considered for entry as a student are that you must:

★ be applying for full-time study,
★ be academically qualified for your proposed course,
★ have an adequate standard of English,
★ have the capacity to cover all your expenses during your entire stay in Australia,
★ be genuinely seeking temporary entry to study only,
★ be of good health.

Students are expected to leave Australia after their study or training and applications by subsidised overseas students to return to Australia as permanent residents will not normally be considered within two years of their departure after study.

Fees and Waiting Time

Fees are charged for all migration applications. Since 1 October 1987, this fee is $225. Sixty dollars or £30 must be enclosed with the initial application and the other $165 paid when requested. All payments must be in Irish pounds, by cheque, money order or postal order made out to 'The Collector General of Public Monies'. There are no exemptions and no refunds.

Waiting time varies with each case and may take longer if there are problems with your case or your qualifications. In general, family reunions for spouses, fiances and parents of Australian citizens get priority and take three to four months, as do Employer Nomination Scheme applications. Other migration applications take 10 to 12 months, unless held up by problems. Working-holiday visas generally take two weeks and holiday visas about a week.

Australia's immigration policy is global and non-discriminatory. There is no set quota for Ireland. The number of temporary visas issued depends on demand and the number of migration visas is set for the world each year. In the current financial year, 1987/88, Australia intends to admit 120,000 people as migrants.

Last year, the Embassy in Dublin fielded 37,000 enquiries. These led to 2,800 migration applications, representing about 6,000 people. About 2,200 migrant and 8,800 temporary visas were issued, a substantial growth over the previous year.

Take heart though, about 70% of those who applied to migrate to Australia were accepted. The failure rate for working holiday and holiday visa applications was even lower, running about 5%.

If you are interested, enquire, if you are eligible, apply.

3 Too Far to Swim – Getting There

The only practical way to Australia from Ireland is to fly. Many Australians over the age of thirty-five have nostalgic memories of the boat voyage from Europe to Australia, but nowadays about the only passenger ships calling at Australian ports are luxury cruises, irregular in their schedules and very expensive.

Over thirty airlines fly to Australia from all over the world. There is competition between them and they try to tempt the traveller either with discounts or with extras like stop-overs at prices so low as to be almost free.

The one you choose will depend on whether you are migrating, going for a working-holiday or just stopping in Australia as part of a round-the-world trip. There are a great many options and things change rapidly. So the advice of a travel agent and lots of research is the order of the day.

None of the airlines fly direct from Dublin. Whatever your choice you will be on a shuttle to some European hub (usually London) and will fly from there to Australia with one or two stops along the way.

Among the top airlines flying to Australia are Qantas (the national airline), British Airways and Singapore Airlines. Malaysian Air Services and Garuda also operate between London and Australia. They all vary in price, conditions, service, comfort and the goodies they offer as incentives to fly with them. MAS and Garuda tend to be cheaper and take longer to get there.

Sample Fares

There is a complex system of peak, high, shoulder and low seasons. For example, this is a current price list for Singapore Airlines for a one-year open return ticket: January £1,129; February £1,071; March, April, May, June £961; July £1,071; August £1,129; September £1,234; October, November, 1-9 December £1,129; 10-23 December £1,234; 24-31 December £1,071.

These are sample fares only, but several things are clear.

The fares dodge up and down throughout the year. The period between March and June should offer the best deal. If you tie yourself down to going in the wrong month you will get well soaked. You are looking at £1,000 for a one-year return. Anything under this, or any extras you can get are a bonus. The fact that your grandfather could have got there for the price of a purloined sheep is no longer relevant!

One Dublin travel agent gave the following sample fares: Dublin to Perth, £869 to £1,142; Sydney, Adelaide, Brisbane and Melbourne, £961 to £1,294. These depend on the season. He also mentioned round-the-world fares with stop-overs in the US, Canada, Hawaii, Fiji, New Zealand, Hong Kong, the Maldives, Singapore, Bangkok, Penang and Australia. The price varies around the £1,000 mark depending on the routes, stop-overs and airlines involved.

Discounts

The basic discounts offered by the major airlines are for Apex, advance purchase and excursion fares. Stop-overs may be limited or banned by taking one of these. Extra savings may be sought by contacting your travel agent, by checking the special advertisements in the national papers and by checking the small ads of magazines like *Private Eye* (the latter for fares from London only).

There are dozens of 'bucket shop' outlets in London that offer very cheap tickets, but it is a lot of extra hassle to check them. Not only do you have to find a bargain, you have to establish the bona fides of the shop as some of them sell rather dubious tickets.

Stop-overs

Stop-overs are a splendid bargain if it suits your plans to take one en route to Australia. One example is the Singapore Airlines deal giving a twin-share room in a leading hotel in Singapore, with breakfast, for just £8 sterling per person. This also includes a free sightseeing tour and discount vouchers for car-hire and shopping.

Bangkok stop-overs start at £20 sterling per person per night, and include the same discounts and vouchers. Both places offer excellent cheap shopping, including (due to their lax or non-existent copyright laws) bargain versions of status symbol watches and other yuppie toys. Unfortunately these often do not live up to their genuine counterparts in performance. If you can bear to be party to doing your favourite millionaire rock star out of a few quid, you can buy cassettes of your favourite music for about a quarter of the Irish price or less. They are pirated of course and while the sound quality is usually OK, the tape itself tends to stretch and fall apart.

You do not need vaccinations for the two stop-overs mentioned above and visas are only required for stays of two weeks and over. If stop-overs are a priority with you, ask about them from the first contact with your travel agent. Otherwise, you may get a bargain fare with no stop-overs allowed.

The Flight

The flight to Australia is fairly gruelling. Depending on stops and transfers, it varies around the 20-hour mark. To keep you happy during the trip, the airlines shove food and drink into you at every opportunity on the way out. They are a bit more restrained on the way back as you are flying through the night (in so far as there is ever a night in the topsy-turvy world of flying halfway around the world).

If you require any special food, such as vegetarian meals, make sure the request goes with your booking and remind the hostesses when you get on the plane. Otherwise, vegetarians may end up with a fistful of peas whipped off the plates of other passengers and a dog-eared cheese sandwich.

There is little else to do but drink and watch the awful films (super-sanitised, so as not to offend anyone). How much of the free drink you lap up depends on your constitution really, but bear in mind the hassles that await you at the far end.

Do not be disconcerted if the passengers give the pilot a round of applause after you land in Australia. It's not that they never expected to make it, it's an Australian tradition.

Most European flights arrive at ungodly hours of the morning, but the airport authorities are kind enough to keep you occupied for the best part of an hour at least. First, you must sit on the plane, while people get on and spray the entire plane and the passengers with aerosols. Far from being a sign that they suspect you all of being lousy, this is to kill disease-carrying insects that may have stowed away in the cabin. Passport and customs checks usually involve queues and more queues.

If you do not have a friend kind or crazy enough to come and fetch you from the airport between 3am and 5am (landing on a Saturday may help here), you will probably just have to sit it out until a reasonable hour of the morning. All major Australian airports are served by airport buses, which are cheaper than getting a taxi. But the chances are you will be in such a state that a taxi will seem like a bargain – at any price. Cheapest of all are ordinary city buses that pass through the airport.

The standard luggage allowance for flights to Australia is 20 kilograms (44lbs), including your one piece of carry-on baggage. You can, of course, pack more than this as long as you are prepared to either dump the excess or pay a hefty surcharge for it if the airline gets sticky. Some airlines, Qantas among them, double the allowance for migrants going to Australia. Even at that, 40kg (88lbs) is not a great deal, so pack carefully.

Bring plenty to read on the plane, perhaps a tape player or anything else you can think of to pass the time. As usual in this imperfect world, carry on your valuables and anything you really cannot afford to have nicked. A spare shirt and socks help you feel better at the far end. Loose clothes are best for comfort and take off your shoes to try and stop your feet from swelling up.

Comfort

Twenty hours without a cigarette is a long time for an addict. You will not be allowed to smoke anywhere except in your own seat, unless there are spare seats in the smoking section, so get a smoking seat if you have to. On the other hand, if you are ambivalent about smoking, you will get an awful lot of other people's smoke anywhere in the smoking section.

There are spectacular views on most flights for those with a window seat. Those who seek extra leg room should beware of the window seat at the mid-wing exit. There is about six feet of space in front of it – but there is also a large escape shute/life raft where your knees would normally go.

It's worth pushing for your favourite seat on such a long flight. The trouble of getting to the airport early to ensure that you get it is well worthwhile. Be absolutely clear about any reconfirmations or check-ins you have to make along the way. Don't wander off too far in airports where you are changing planes and remember that the duty-free shops in these transit areas have a captive market and prices to match.

One problem with cheaper airlines is that they may try handing you a ready-printed boarding card, giving you no choice in where you sit when you have to transfer in a dazed scrum early in the morning.

4 Your Swag – What to Bring

Referees and contact addresses

You need referees for almost every rental transaction in Australia (even hiring a TV). Get some names and addresses of people living in the area where you intend to live who would be prepared to be your referees. The companies which request this will rarely make contact with the referees, they are only assurance as to your identity. Even if you have no intention of seeing these people, their presence and status in a society in which you are an alien will help. Irish referees, no matter how impressive, are too remote to be of much use to these companies.

Bring as many addresses of possible useful contacts as you can get hold of too, especially people working in similar fields. Most people will help a fellow traveller or new arrival, even if it is only to give advice over the phone. People resident in Australia and fellow Paddies are both useful in different ways.

Certified Copies of Qualifications

Photocopies of *all* professional qualifications are generally unacceptable in Australia without certification. This applies more to the State and Federal organisations with which you may have to register than private employers. You have a choice: bring originals of all documents relating to your trade training, skills, educational and professional qualifications and take care of them, or have your photocopies certified (Migrants bring originals). Certification can be done by a Justice of the Peace or Notary Public in Australia. There is not usually a charge, all they do is affix a stamp to say they are genuine. It would be far easier to have your copies stamped by the organisation involved, (university or whatever) before you leave. If this is not possible, a letter from the relevant organisation stating your course of study and qualification should suffice. Go to the student records office.

Curriculum Vitae
(Also known as cv, work history or resumé)
Bring a few copies of your Irish cv, but it is better to have a

new one typed with your Australian phone number and address. It may also be useful to give more information about the nature of your work and experience than you would here, as Australian employers may be unfamiliar with the Irish terms of job description and the companies or organisations you mention. Research the Australian terminology in your field (perhaps just by looking at job ads). If your address will change frequently, arrange it so typed labels may be stuck over the old address, or have it all retyped.

Typing can be done quickly and professionally by any secretarial agency in Australia, use the Yellow Pages. ($12-18, depending on length.)

Bank Statements
Bring any credit references which will help you to establish credit in Australia. If you are leaving funds here take a statement of these, also make sure you have receipts for any assets you have already transferred such as bank accounts you have opened. Don't forget to take advantage of the tax exemptions for people non-resident in Ireland and sign a declaration of non-residency if you are leaving money in an account here. There is no point in paying tax in two countries!

Other useful documents
Here follows a list which may or may not apply to you:
Where possible, bring originals.
Work references, driving licence, birth certificate, marriage licence, insurance and VHI policies (arrange a transfer of these), vaccination certificates, lenses and prescription for contact lens and glasses.
People with special medical problems (eg: diabetes) or who need special medication should bring the necessary doctor's notes and perhaps the name and address of a specialist in Australia. Finally, don't forget your passport—it's a long way home.

Recognition of Qualifications

Professional: As standards of education and training vary from country to country, your qualifications may not be recognised by the equivalent Australian body. This is obviously most important when, as with nurses and teachers, you may not practice your profession in State-organised institutions without prior approval and registration with the appropriate

State Department. Private employers may not be as fussy, or may simply assume your qualifications are valid. Do watch out for this problem, even some highly regarded qualifications are unacceptable in Australia. Requirements for States vary, but generally, if you have managed to register with one State, the others will accept you too.

You can check either with the Australian Embassy in Dublin (for migrants this should be done automatically), or the Council on Overseas Professional Qualifications, based in the Department of Immigration, Local Government and Ethnic Affairs' Central Office in Canberra.

Nurses may write to Canberra for an assessment of qualifications form, return it, and have it sent back to them. The relevant body is: Australian Nursing Assessment Council, PO Box 390, Kingston, ACT 2604. They can also go through their own hospitals or through an Bord Altranais.

The address for all other professional qualifications is: Council on Overseas Professional Qualifications, Benjamin Offices, Chan Street, Belconnen, ACT 2617 Tel (062) 641111

Trade Qualifications: Tradesmen who are migrating will have their qualifications assessed here before they go. Sometimes they will have to satisfy further trade test requirements before they can be accepted as fully licensed tradesmen. For some areas of work in the plumbing and electrical trades, you need a licence issued by the relevant State or Territory Authority. In Australia trade qualifications can be assessed by the Department of Employment and Industrial Relations in Canberra, (DEIR), 1 Farrell Place, Canberra, ACT 2601. Bring your tools with you. If they are heavy and bulky, migrants should send them surface. Buying good new ones will cost a fortune.

Clothes and personal gear

Clothes
This is not an exhaustive list, but ideas based on experience. Bear in mind the kind of work you intend to do, and the climate where you are going to live. A reasonably smart outfit will be useful for interviews, job and flat hunting. If you intend to be a waiter/ress, black trousers/skirt, white blouse/shirt

and black or white shoes would be handy.

Cheap light summer clothing and underwear are better quality and cheaper in Ireland, shoes likewise. All cheap shoes in Australia are synthetic and short-lived. Don't forget *some* warm clothes – at least one heavy sweater, trousers and a weather-proof jacket. It does rain in every major city; Melbourne and Tasmania especially have cold, wet winters. Cotton sweatshirts are very useful for chilly evenings in warmer places. Buy cotton and natural fabrics in preference to synthetic ones, they are more comfortable in hot weather and easier to look after. At the same time don't overload with clothing, your mobility is important. Everything you can buy here can be bought there. Unless you are emigrating, or prepared to drag heavy luggage around, travel light and buy as you go. Suggested list for a minimal wardrobe:

Women
Suit (perhaps), skirts, blouses (work clothes)
2 summer dresses
2 pairs trousers, one pair jeans
1 pair shorts, some t-shirts, 2 sweatshirts
1 rainproof jacket, 1 wool jersey
1 smart outfit
2 pairs smart shoes
2 pairs sandals
1 pair walking shoes/runners
Underwear
Swimming costume
Tracksuit

Men
Jacket, shirts, trousers, ties (work clothes)
2 pairs light trousers, one pair jeans
1 pair shorts, some t-shirts, sweatshirts
1 rainproof jacket, 2 jerseys (useful for work if cold)
1 suit or smart outfit
2 pairs shoes
1 pair sandals (flipflops are cheaper and cooler)
1 pair walking shoes/runners
Underwear
Swimming trunks
Tracksuit

Personal Gear

A sleeping bag or bedclothes of some kind will definitely be needed, both for holidays and your own accommodation. Bedlinen, blankets and continental quilts (dunas) are more expensive in Oz, sleeping bags are similar in price. Beware of cheap chainstore bags, they can be too light, and shrink. The Embassy recommends that migrants, especially ones with families, send bedding by air to help set up a home.

A radio cassette player can be useful in the first lonely days. It can help you get acclimatised to the ads, shops and language. Don't forget a few of your favourite Irish tapes. Cassettes cost about $15 and while the range is similar to here, they have probably never heard of your very favourite band. A travelling iron may be a worthwhile investment to make you less crumpled for that first interview.

Electrical items are slightly more expensive in Australia (Bottom of the range radio/cassette player $120, new iron $38 plus, secondhand iron $10), so bring your own or buy duty free on the way. Research prices if you intend to buy duty free, some airports (Singapore) are expensive.

Check the voltage. The standard electrical supply in Australia is 240V AC (50 HZ), the same as here. Cut the plugs off before you go and make sure you can put the Australian ones on, they are completely different.

One item of almost unlimited usefulness is a Swiss-army style knife. A good one can be your instant tool kit for changing plugs, extracting cassettes from tape players and other household chores. In your cold, bare flat it means you will never be without a sharp knife, a tin opener or, of course, a cork screw.

If you are going away for a long time, maybe intending to settle, think about sentimental items. Photos, any personal mementoes and items you are particularly fond of may seem silly and unnecessary. Their value will increase with distance.

What people wear (the clothes to choose)

To generalise hugely, female work clothes are reasonably smart (dresses, suits, blouses and skirts). Women still wear very traditional 'feminine' clothes to work. Jeans and trousers are not so common, but minis, sexy slits and skimpy sundresses are noticeably more popular than in Ireland. (The climate? Irish modesty?) Male work clothes tend to be more casual, with trousers (not jeans) and short-sleeved shirts the norm. Suits are rarely worn, except in the upper levels of conservative businesses. Ties are not obligatory, but make a surprisingly good impression. In summer, men sometimes wear knee-length socks, plain long shorts, light shoes, shirt and tie. This looks cute and school-boyish, but is not popular with the under-40s.

Casual clothes are exactly that. Standard leisure wear is shorts or tracksuit pants and t-shirt for both male and female. Flip-flops (thongs) are also common. Many bars use 'No shorts, no thongs' as a means of restricting entry – shows how popular they are!

Followers of fashion will find clothes and styles old-fashioned, or just different. This is because the season there is either a year ahead or a year behind the season here, and what you have seen in the shops in Ireland all last summer will reappear all next summer in Australia.

What not to bring – Quarantine and Customs

Vaccinations and health precautions
Travellers to Australia may be required to undergo a medical check on arrival. Those with suspected infectious diseases are isolated and placed in quarantine accommodation. New arrivals must report to a quarantine office if they suffer from illness or disease within 14 days. You will be given a slip of paper about this when you arrive.

You do not need any vaccinations for entry to Australia unless you have travelled through or landed at a place within a yellow fever infected zone, within six days before arrival. For the yellow fever requirement (zones include Central Africa, Central and South America) you must have a current yellow fever vaccination certificate, unless you are less than 12 months old.

Areas where typhoid, cholera, malaria, etc., are endemic include most of Asia. Aircraft refuelling stops do not necessitate vaccination, nor do many stop-overs, but you *must* check this with your travel agent. Obviously, if you are spending any length of time in Asia on your way to Australia, it is a good idea to have a whole range of vaccinations anyway.

Migrants

Parents of children under 13 are advised to have them immunised against diptheria, whooping cough, poliomyelitis and tetanus, just as in Ireland. If you are migrating with a family this can be done after arrival, at school or local clinics. Similarly, teenage girls should be immunised against rubella. If your children have already been immunised, it would be useful to bring the certificates with you.

AIDS Test

A compulsory AIDS test for all visitors to Australia has been mentioned by the present government. As yet there are no definite plans for its introduction and it seems unlikely to ever come into effect. What might happen if you tested positive under this proposed scheme is not clear.

Quarantine

There are many prohibited goods which you cannot bring into Australia. Obviously narcotic and hallucinogenic drugs are a total no-no. Less obviously, *all* foods of animal origin, including meat and dairy products, are forbidden entry unless given a special permit from the quarantine service. Think twice about that present of Irish smoked salmon for your relatives. If you have any of the following items, prior approval must be obtained before departure:

1. Cats, dogs and other small animals. These can only be admitted under stringent conditions. A prior import permit is required and a period of quarantine necessary. This will probably cost more than your own airfare. Buy a new one when you get there.
2. Cultures, organisms, animal semen and ova.
3. Live plants, cuttings and bulbs.
4. Firearms and weapons.
5. Cordless telephones.

Do not bring birds, feathers or poultry products, eggs or egg products, aquatic life or fish (including salmon!), plants, crop seed, live insects or soil. Dairy products, including cheese. Meat, including salami, sausages and canned meat. Fresh fruit and vegetables.

Goods manufactured from protected species of wildlife, including skins, feathers, bones, articles of apparel and accessories such as handbags, shoes, trophies and ornaments are also subject to restriction. Finally, and this is a sneaky one, do not bring food items left over from the plane. Bins are thoughtfully provided for those who forget, or just can't resist those handy sachets of sugar.

The following must be shown to quarantine officials on arrival: Holy water, baby foods, nuts, wooden, bamboo and cane articles, furred skins, unfinished leather goods.

Customs
The usual duty-free allowances are available for goods for personal use. You are allowed one litre of any alcohol (beer, wine or spirits), 250 cigarettes or grams of tobacco, and other goods to a total value of $400 (duty free). You should keep all receipts. Persons under 18 may only bring in $200 worth of duty-free goods.

Visitors to Australia, resident overseas, may also bring in a variety of other goods, so long as they re-export them. You may have to pay a security, or sign a declaration that the goods will be taken out of the country again. Your yacht, car and caravan come into this category. Any unaccompanied baggage and goods are liable to duty and sales tax, unless you are migrating.

Migrants
Migrants to Australia may bring in practically all their personal and household possessions, duty-free, accompanied or sent separately, provided they have been owned and used for 12 months or more before departure. This is obviously a difficult one to prove. If they have not been used for a year before departure, they may be liable for duty, these include:

Binoculars, typewriters, cameras, personal sporting requisites and bicycles (non-motorised),
household appliances such as washing machines, refrigerators etc.
household linen and bedding such as sheets, pillowcases, blankets, quilts etc.
furniture, including pianos, radiograms, television sets, stereo equipment, projectors etc.

Procedure
On the plane or on arrival you will be given a form to complete. This is a series of questions which amounts to a list of declared goods, if you tick the 'yes' boxes. These will probably

be inspected by customs officials. Any items in your baggage may be examined, declared or not. The customs officials are more zealous than here. Do not try smuggling and, if in doubt at all, check with a customs or quarantine official. Penalties for not doing so are heavy: up to $50,000 fine or ten years in jail. A lot of detailed information is available from the Embassy, useful leaflets are:

'What about my departure?'

'Australia. A protected place.'

'Australian Customs Information, all passengers.'

You can also write directly to the authorities in Australia if you have a special problem. Make sure you get the appropriate authority, as this area is a bureaucratic maze. The addresses of all authorities can be found in the Useful Addresses section. Ultimate authority is held by the Comptroller-General of the Australian Customs Service and his collectors at the port of entry.

5 A Place to Stay

Temporary shelter

Having struggled through the queues at the airport, your first priority must be a place to stay. If you are lucky enough to have somewhere you can stay for a while, use it. Be careful though, if the address is far (more than 15 kilometres) from the city centre. The advantages of free friendly facilities will be outweighed by problems of transport, especially if you want to use it as a base for job-hunting and finding long-term accommodation. Do not outstay your welcome. More than a week – no matter how nice you are – is too much for most people!

If you cannot use a friend or relative, all cities (and most towns) have a range of cheap accommodation. Hostels like those of the Youth Hostel Association or Backpackers (with prices from about $7 per night for dormitory beds) provide a meeting place and useful contacts for flatshares, employment and car buying.

YMCA and YWCA hostels are more upmarket and more expensive ($18 and up for a single room). The rooms are nicer and the Ys often give weekly rates, and have cheap restaurants and social facilities (gym, television lounge) in the building. Some Ys do not mind what sex you are, others allow couples and a few are strictly for either men or women. The Melbourne YWCA, which takes men and couples as well as women, is particularly nice, but pricey.

A room of your own, or a locked luggage store is useful if you have just arrived with all your gear. Use the hostel safe, if they have one, for valuables, and keep an eye on your possessions.

Cheap accommodation, and particularly hostels, gets booked out, so phone from the airport. Choose somewhere central, close to the main bus and rail terminals if you are going to be looking for work or long-term accommodation.

After hostels, there are private hotels. The cheaper ones (about $18 for a single room) are often seedy and close to railway stations. They too, often give a weekly rate, but tend to be less welcoming to the newly arrived.

Motels are usually expensive ($25 and up, with doubles cheaper) and are often out of the city centre.

All airports provide some tourist information. Even when the information stand is closed, you can pick up free maps and 'what's on' guides. They contain all sorts of ads for places to stay.

There is a short sample list of hostels and private hotels in the 'Useful Addresses' section at the back of the book.

Long-term accommodation

You have three main choices in this area: renting a flat or house, sharing a house, or living in serviced/holiday apartments. It is reasonable to expect to take at least a week to find somewhere. You will need a street directory (about $20, but worth it), bus timetables and route maps and easy access to a telephone, to help with your search.

Flat, House, Share or Holiday Apartments? Your choice depends largely on your circumstances and on how long you intend to stay. A flat requires a large initial investment of time and money – unless you want to live on the floor and eat tins of beans. Sharing is easier and cheaper, if you don't mind risking strange housemates. Holiday apartments will be equipped and have short leases, if any, but will be more expensive. A selection of sample prices follows this section. The rents vary with the season, exact location, and the facilities offered, so shop around.

Having decided on the type of long-term accommodation you want, pick two or three likely suburbs. Here advice from someone who knows the city on undesirable areas and local social life is invaluable. Bear in mind transport, closeness to the city centre and local shopping. Most Australian cities are very suburbanised and rely on huge shopping centres which are difficult to get to without a car. Limiting yourself to researching and looking in a few parts of town will make the whole business much easier.

All cities have certain days on which the bulk of the accommodation advertising appears. Usually, it is in the quality morning paper on Wednesdays and Saturdays. Gear your hunt to these days because the columns can be a bit bare on the other days. Allow yourself a day or two to get your bearings and an idea of rent levels before starting to look in earnest.

Some likely areas that balance cost and comfort are:

Sydney: Bondi, Coogee, Paddington and Potts Point in the eastern suburbs, Redfern (cheap but rough). Places like Kirribilli, on the harbour, are beautiful but expensive. Avoid the western suburbs.

Melbourne: Carlton, Brunswick and Fitzroy (all becoming more expensive), South Yarra. Anywhere near the university is good for food and shopping.

Perth: Subiaco, anywhere near Kings Park, Maylands (roughish), Rivervale, Victoria Park, South Perth (expensive) and Como. Avoid East Perth, Balga, Northbridge.

Brisbane: Quite difficult to find flats here. Many people opt for long hostel stays. Try Kangaroo Point and St Lucia.

Adelaide: North Adelaide (expensive), Glenelg, West Beach, Henley Beach.

What to look for

Try to find some where with:

1) A telephone. Very useful for job hunting. Employers are not impressed by calls from noisy phone boxes. New friendships are also hard to make without one. Pay phones tend to be few and far between in the suburbs. Having a phone already installed saves time and money.

2) Washing machine. It sounds extravagant but will be cheaper than using a laundromat for any length of time. Many places have shared laundries.

3) Flyscreens and a balcony. These are not essential, but make life easier in any of the hotter areas such as Perth, Darwin and Brisbane.

4) Cockroaches: Look for signs of these pests and before you move in spray the place thoroughly. (Baygon is a surface spray which lasts for about three months and costs approximately $5). Relatively harmless, they do infest food and make unpleasant housemates, especially for those from the Northern Hemisphere who are unused to their company.

Flats and Houses

Possible sources: Newspapers, local estate agencies.

Useful jargon
Flat = unit
Bachelor apartment = bedsit.
Home unit, townhouse = two storey flat.   .
Duplex = expensive flat, often with garden, (yard).
Part furnished = very bare essentials.
Furnished = just about, with beds, fridge, cooker.
Fully furnished = furniture and kitchen, but usually no crockery, pans, etc. or bedclothes.

Payment
You will have to pay a bond (deposit) and two weeks, at least, rent in advance. Estate agents will also require a letting fee, (usually 10% of first month's rent) and Government Stamp Duty (a fixed tax, about $4). The latter two are sometimes ignored by private landlords.

The bond is usually one month's rent. So, for example, if you choose a typical one-bedroomed flat with a gas cooker in Sydney, which costs $110 a week, you will have to pay $440 bond, two weeks' rent in advance ($220), a letting fee of $44 and $4 stamp duty. This adds up to $708. Include the deposits for gas and electricity, about $110 in total, reconnection charges for these services of about $40 altogether, phone reconnection, about $35, and basic kitchen equipment – which is very rarely supplied – at a minimum $25. You are looking at a total expenditure of about $918. This is assuming that you have your own bedclothes. Of course,the $440 bond should be returned, but a flat is still a major capital outlay. It is best if you can find some friends or travelling companions to share the initial costs with. All of these items are dealt with in more detail, section by section.

Bond
The bond should be receipted and registered with the Rental Bond Board by your landlord. It will be returned to you by the landlord at the end of the lease. Landlord and lessees must sign a release form. Some or all of it may be withheld if the property has been damaged. In the case of dispute your property inventory or condition report will be important. (See below). If you terminate (break) your lease early you are likely to be charged a percentage of the loss of rent or the cost of readvertising by an estate agency. This will be taken from

the bond. A way round this may be to agree with your landlord to release the bond money in lieu of your final month's rent. To do this you fill in a special form available from the Rental Bond Board and some banks.

Property Condition Report

Most estate agencies and landlords will produce a written record of inspection stating the condition of the property when you move in. This must be signed by you and returned soon after possession (usually within seven days). Check the accuracy of this, item by item, room by room and if necessary query it. It may be the saving of your bond money.

Lease

Usually six months minimum, sometimes twelve. Read the lease carefully as many of the subsections (parties, washing on balconies etc) can safely be ignored, but others, hidden in the small print, may be important. Make sure you are clear about the notice period you must give if breaking the lease, (usually one month or rental period) and the possibility of extending it should you wish to. Your tenancy (period of rent payments and date for vacation of the property) will usually date from signature of the lease, but some landlords may allow you to post-date until you actually move in. This could save a few days' rent.

Your lease will contain standard clauses about responsibility for repair. This will usually be covered by the landlord but beware of mechanical items such as fridges and washing machines. Sort out who pays the repairman and, if you do, make sure the machines work before you move in. It sounds obvious (and difficult to do if the electricity isn't connected!) but a minor oversight can become a major problem in rented accommodation.

Once you have given notice to terminate your lease, or it is nearing the end of the agreed period, the landlord can show it to prospective tenants. This is embarrassing (who wants prospective tenants viewing you in bed on a Saturday morning?) but unavoidable.

Two copies of the lease must be signed by both lessor and lessee(s) and witnessed. You keep a copy, the landlord the other.

Always make sure you have a lease – forms for private

landlords are available from stationers – and receipts for all payments: deposit (if any), bond, rent paid in advance, letting fee and regular rental payments.

Telephone, Gas and Electricity

These should be disconnected (if this has not already been done) and reconnected with accounts in your name on the date you move in. This can easily be arranged by telephone, in advance. Deposits are needed for gas and electricity in some States (payable at the local office, within 7/14 days of connection $50-60) and you will also have to pay a reconnection fee (in your first bill, $20 approximately for gas and electricity, $35 for telephone).

Altogether, you can expect to need about $150 for provision of and payment for services over and above rent and everything else that has already been paid to the landlord or estate agent.

Costs for services are quite reasonable – certainly cheaper than their equivalents here. For example, electricity averages less than $2 a day for three people with washing machine, fridge, tumble dryer, cooker, instant water heater, etc. Using gas for cooking and water heating amounts to less than $1 a day. This will vary with differing state charges and climate.

Telephone costs, including rental, are approximately $40 quarterly. Local calls are about 15 cents. The country's size does result in huge bills for interstate calls, and its remoteness means *massive* bills for international calls. Resist the temptation to do an ET too often. An ascending scale, with mindboggling distances and charges is in the front of the phone book. Installing a working telephone from scratch will cost five times as much as a simple reconnection.

Dealing with Landlords

There is competition for most half-way reasonable flats and there is a definite bias in most cities against new arrivals and the unemployed. Estate agents will ask you to fill out an application form. Details of referees, bank accounts, credit cards and employment are requested (and given the third degree). Dress and appearance are also taken into consideration. Private landlords will usually interview you with the same criteria in mind. If you haven't got a job, proving that you have enough money is all-important. It may be worth taking a bedsit or rather grotty flat to begin with, while you become established.

As with all flathunting, speed is essential. Get up early, scan the ads, phone likely places, get the addresses and arrange viewing times. Use your street directory to locate them and visit several. If you like one, snap it up. Be ready with all the information and have enough for a deposit in hand. Around $50 should suffice to secure a place until you arrange a time for the signing of the lease and payment of the balance.

Sample Prices

A sample list of accommodation prices for 1987, weekly rents:

Sydney   Australian Dollars
Bedsitter/one-bedroomed flat $70 to $140
Two-bedroomed unit/flat $95 and up
House $120 and up

Melbourne
Bedsitter/one bedroomed flat $50 to $120
Two-bedroomed unit/flat $80 and up
House $100 and up

Adelaide
Bedsitter/one bedroomed flat $50 to $120
Two-bedroomed unit/flat $75 and up
House $90 and up

Perth
Bedsitter/one-bedroomed flat $50 to $110
Two-bedroomed unit/flat $80 and up
House $100 and up

Brisbane
Bedsitter/one-bedroomed flat $50 to $80
Two-bedroomed unit/flat $60 to $130
House $80 and up

You may find places that are cheaper than these, usually in unpopular suburbs, or very far from the city centre. An awful lot will be more expensive. Unfurnished flats are often far cheaper and easier to find than furnished ones. Houses are scarce on the rental market and are always more expensive. Sydney is the most expensive city in which to find accommodation, Melbourne and Adelaide are slightly cheaper and Brisbane and Perth are the cheapest of all.

As you can see, moving into a flat or any rented accommodation of your own is an expensive and time-consuming business, possibly only worth considering for a long stay.

Sharing

You may find housesharing a far cheaper and easier proposition than having a place of your own. You will meet people and perhaps make some friends. On the other hand. . . they could become enemies for life. If the advertisement sounds weird, chances are the people are also weird. Use your judgement and make sure you meet *all* the people living in the house. In this context 'Broad minded person wanted' often means the other occupants may be gay.

Sources: Newspapers, workmates, hostel noticeboards.

Payment: Varies. The ad will say if a bond is required and if rent includes bills. If not, you may have to pay a deposit towards future gas and electricity payments. You pay rent in advance, usually two weeks.

Shares will cost anything from $45 a week upwards. Average payment is $60 to $80 a week. This works out more expensive than sharing a flat with friends, but you do not have the huge initial expenses of a large bond, equipping the place and reconnecting services. Nor will you be tied to a long lease.

For example, an average house-share in Melbourne, which costs $70 a week in rent, will only require an initial payment of $140 (two weeks' rent in advance), plus a bond if necessary ($280) and perhaps a deposit towards future bills of $100. This adds up to $520, but it is easy enough to find a share which does not require a bond or a deposit.

Lease

You should not have to sign one but find out who is on the lease and its duration. *Do* write and sign an agreement on the notice period needed for you to vacate the premises. This should also stipulate the terms under which you get your bond back if relevant, and any rent paid in advance. You do not want to end up on the streets – penniless – at 3 am, after a blazing row.

Dealing with shares

Here, advice is similar for flathunting. Get on the phone fast and arrange a viewing time/interview. Be prepared for leading questions like 'Do you like loud music?' you are hanged if you do and hanged if you do not.

Shop around and do not get pressurised into taking somewhere. Most house-shares have a stack of people to interview and will call you back having seen them all. Be wary of the ones that have no other applications! Be crystal clear on the system of payment of bills, especially the telephone, before you move in.

Holiday or Serviced Apartments

This is a generic term covering anything from bedsits to luxury apartments. Designed for short-term occupation, their advantage is that they are fully equipped and will have a short lease or none at all. Possible sources are tourist 'What's on' guides, newspaper ads and estate agents. Payment may include a bond and rent in advance inclusive of gas, electricity and other services. You pay a flat rate for all it provides, hence 'serviced' apartments. They tend to be expensive (50% more than a standard flat) but may be useful if you have an uncertain time scale.

An alternative would be to find a hostel with cooking facilities, or a cheap hotel with 'light cooking facilities', (usually a kettle, toaster and fridge) and organise a weekly rate.

Neither of these is easy to jobhunt from and they are not exactly homely. You will always end up paying more if you stay in one of these places for any length of time. Some examples of these can be found in the Useful Addresses section.

The Cost of Living

Accommodation

The embassy guide reckons that you will spend one-quarter to one-third of your weekly income on accommodation. This will vary of course with the city and may be far less if you share with other people. Average costs for an individual in a shared flat would be $50 to $60.

Food

Food, living well, with regular steak, roasts and fish, using markets and cheap vegetable shops, should come to about $30 a week per person, or less. Again, sharing is far cheaper than buying for one. Suburban shopping centres and vegetable markets are far cheaper than city-centre supermarkets. Australia goes in for large-scale packaging and discounts for bulk purchases. Half-sheep and huge packages of things are very cheap indeed, but will be almost impossible to use unless you have a big household or a freezer.

Recent figures indicate that the average household (man, woman and 2.2 children) spends about 21% of the average weekly wage on food each week. Prices do not vary tremendously from city to city, but fresh fruit and vegetables are obviously cheaper closer to source.

Transport

Public transport is quite cheap in comparison to Ireland. Weekly bus and rail tickets are good value for commuters. Many cities have a zoning system with blanket increases for each zone – making it more expensive than our stage system if you live just inside a zone boundary. Regular commuters could expect to pay between $10 and $12 to get to work all week, and get around at weekends on public transport.

People socialising at night, who are without a car, will inevitably have to use taxis unless they are prepared to go home before public transport stops, which can be quite early, especially on Sunday nights. Taxis are expensive if used on a regular basis. In 1984, the average household spent 16.3% of its income on transport.

Most people should be able to live easily and cover expenses with about $120 a week, leaving lots of money left over from the average wage for holidays, eating out, entertainment and, of course, alcohol, cigarettes and such like.

For detailed, up-to-date information on the cost of living, see the Commonwealth Bank's useful half-yearly survey, available from the bank or in the Embassy in Dublin.

6 Yakka (Work) – And how to find it

After a nasty lurch over 10% in the early 1980s, unemployment has dropped back to a little over 8%. That's a good deal less than half the Irish figure, but is still higher than what Australia has traditionally been accustomed to. Unemployment is seen as an important national problem, but there are still a great many opportunities. The crammed situations vacant columns of Australian newspapers come as a happy shock to many Irish people.

On the other hand, Australia is not the land of milk and honey. Do not expect to walk into an easy, well-paid job. Do not go at all unless you have reason to expect that you will get work. There are thousands of bright, educated, skilled Australians to compete with you. You will have to get on your bike and find a job.

From this end

Whether you are hoping to emigrate to Australia, going for a working-holiday, or stopping off on a round-the-world trip, you should put some preparation into seeking work in Australia. You are unlikely to be head-hunted by an Australian firm if you sit quietly in Rathangan or in Rathmines.

Those whose visa depends on having a firm job offer, will have to go to the most effort. If a relative can arrange a job for you, so much the better. Make it easier for him or her by supplying several copies of your cv and qualifications. Those who do not have a sponsor to do the leg-work, will have to use every avenue to find out about jobs in Australia and put a good deal of work into getting a firm job offer.

An employer is unlikely to go through the complex procedures and paperwork of sponsorship unless your skills or profession are in great demand. A company may not make you a firm job offer, but instead express interest in seeing you on arrival. If this leaves you with a visa problem, you could visit Australia on a temporary visa to follow up firm openings.

A good first step is to visit the Embassy library in Dublin, which is open weekdays except Wednesday from 8.30 am to 12.30 pm (like the visa section). There is a selection of Australian newspapers with ads that will give you a good idea of the demand for your skills. There is also a classified telephone directory for each city. You can gather addresses from these for letters of enquiry. Even if an advertised job is not exactly what you are qualified for, it may be worth writing and expressing an interest in similar openings. Use friends, those in Australia and those who have returned, to get information about your field and the likely openings in it. Look up the trade union or professional organisation covering your occupation and enquire about the situation from it.

Having got at least expressions of interest, it might be worth your while to go to Australia as a visitor to pursue openings. If you can afford it, this is one of the best ways of strengthening the interest of a potential employer in you. You will also get a taste of Australian life that may help you make up your mind on whether you really want to move there.

Head-Hunting

Major Australian companies sometimes come to London to recruit people for vacancies they cannot fill at home. Get a friend in London in a similar line of work to your own to look out for notices of such visits. The designated employment list issued by the Embassy is a rough guide to the fields in which such active recruitment may be taking place.

One of the advantages of being head-hunted like this is that your future employer will often pay your fare and offer some sort of relocation allowance. This is usually set against your period of work with the company. If you leave within a certain period you will have to pay back a proportion of their investment in you.

Job directories and employment agencies

There are other ways of getting in touch with potential employers. One is to buy a jobs directory of some sort. These are usually culled from the classified phone book and are lists of companies arranged under their areas of business. If you are too far from Dublin to get in to the Embassy to search the telephone directories yourself, or simply cannot be bothered, one of these may be a good investment.

Find out about the trade journal associated with your occupation in Australia and take out a subscription. If you intend to apply directly for jobs advertised in such a journal, you will have to pay for an airmail subscription. The closing dates for jobs will be long past if you reply on surface mail. If, on the other hand, you just want to test the water, surface mail may do.

There is an agency in Britain that will list potential employers for you, city by city. Leesons Employment and Accommodation Data Service can be contacted at 4 Cranley Road, Newbury Park, Ilford, Essex IG1 6AG.

You could also try Australian employment agencies. In the Embassy library list the agencies in the city that interest you. Give priority to any that specialise in your line of work. Of course, they will be more interested in people with skills that are in strong demand in Australia.

If you are a graduate, visit the graduate careers and appointments office and check the files on Australia. One of the people who work there may have some special contacts in Australia. You could also check with your faculty office, if the faculty is a tightly knit one, about whether any recent graduates have gone to Australia. If so, you could contact them for advice relevant to your field of work.

If you know, or even know of, any Australians in Ireland working in jobs like the ones you are interested in, you could ask them for advice. If you work for an international company, enquire about Australian associates, branches or subsidiaries and the possibility of transferring.

In Australia

There are six main ways of finding work: The Commonwealth Employment Service, newspaper advertisements, employment agencies, your union, casual enquiries, friends and contacts. Jobhunting procedures are quite similar to those that apply in Ireland, but there are some important variations.

The CES

The recommended first step is to register with the Commonwealth Employment Service (CES). This government organisation is rather like Manpower, but unlike it, it actually has jobs on offer. There should be an office near you, but it is best to go either to the main city branch or to one that specialises in your line of work, if there is one. Check the government section at the front of the telephone directory.

Register there, giving details of your experience and qualifications. You will have an interview, which will give you some useful advice and suggestions. The CES will then try to match your skills with jobs that are available and will contact you when this has been done. You go ahead and apply for the job in the normal way. In the meantime, call in and check the CES notice boards every second day. Interesting vacancies will come up and disappear just as quickly. The CES is also the first step towards getting the dole, but Irish citizens just off the plane are generally not entitled to it.

Private Employment Agencies
Try the private employment agencies too. Find them in the classified telephone directory. They also often advertise in newspapers. The agency will usually ask you in for a short interview before putting you on their books. Here previous experience is all-important. Do your best to impress the agency and its staff will pass on the good impression to potential employers. With large numbers on their books, they will only pass on those people who have impressed them with their capacity to deal efficiently with an unfamiliar company, possibly in crisis, with little help from anyone on the job. This particularly refers to short-term 'overload' type jobs.

Rates and conditions of pay vary from agency to agency. Find out about charges for using their service and whether you or the employer pays. If, as with most short-term relief work, the agency is paying you directly, try to negotiate a reasonable rate. It is not unusual for the agency to pass on only 50% of what the company is paying for your service. The keener the agency is to have you, the better your bargaining position.

Newspaper Advertisements
Find out the main newspaper used for job advertising and the days job ads appear in your city. Like housing ads, it is usually Wednesday and Saturday in the quality morning paper, but, for example, *The Australian* carries a monthly computer supplement crammed with computer jobs. Monday is often good for part-time work. Get up early, or better still,

get the early edition of the paper, which is available at the paper's offices from about 11 pm the night before. You will need time to scan the mass of job ads. Circle those that interest you and put them in order of choice.

Be pushy and get an interview. Unlike Ireland, it is no harm to call about a job even if you are asked to apply in writing. Perhaps you can get a more detailed job description or the name of the person to whom your application should be sent. Maybe you will even be asked to come for an interview straight away. Speed is essential. Get on the phone fast. The hours between 8.00 am and 11.00 am are crucial. Be ready to start calling as soon as the office opens, and keep trying. For casual jobs, interviews will only be given to the first few callers, or even to the first person who rings.

Casual Enquiries – Just Walk In
It is surprising how many people find work by simply walking in and asking for it. This is especially true of jobs in the hospitality and catering trades, hotels, hospitals, bars and shops. Dress smartly, list the addresses of likely places and set off with your cv and details of your work experience at the ready. Ask for the personnel manager or whoever is in charge of staff recruitment. Even if they have no vacancies, they may put you on to somewhere which has, or keep you on file for future work. Be confident and sell yourself.

You can try this too with longer term 'career' jobs. List the companies that might employ people like you. Write in 'cold' to the personnel manager (call first to get his or her name) and offer to come for a chat. Again, even if they do not have immediate openings, they may keep you in mind.

Using Friends and Contacts
Here the addresses you gathered before you left home will be a big help. People on the spot should be able to tell you of casual work that is going and companies that are looking for staff. Check hostel notice boards and sound out people you meet in hostels. Strictly casual work that is very short-term goes more often by notice boards and word of mouth than by advertising. A few examples we came across were: packing books in a Sydney warehouse ($80 a day, through a friend of a friend), surveying traffic in Melbourne ($40 a day, university notice board), shifting bricks on a Perth building site ($70

a day, through a friend on the job). Keep your ear to the ground and tell everyone you meet that you are looking for work. Some construction gangs and firms are predominantly Irish. If you are looking for this sort of work, collect names and contacts from friends and in Irish hang-outs.

Trade Unions
If the work you are interested in is heavily unionised, like journalism or building, either transfer your union member-ship or join the equivalent union in Australia. It is worth bearing in mind that union dues may be lower in Australia. Call in to the union office and ask about any service that they have for placing their members in jobs. Even if they do not maintain a file of jobs on offer, the officials may help put you on the right track. Some will even let you use the office as a jobhunting base.

If you are a union member and are going into a unionised job, check what the terms of the relevant pay award are. National pay awards cover a great many jobs in Australia and lay down conditions on sick pay and holiday pay as well as weekly or hourly rates.

Union membership is very high and you may find that you are moving from a non-union job in Ireland to a unionised one in Australia. The closed shop operates in many areas. If you are offered a job in a place in which everyone else is a union member, it is probably wiser to join. A foreigner, newly arrived, is not in a great position for making a heroic stand for the right not to join a union.

Using the telephone
It should be obvious by now how important it is to have a telephone when you are looking for work. Many Australian companies have an aversion to using the post (even though it delivers next day in every city). They will even send out couriers with messages rather than post a letter. You make it that bit easier for them by having a telephone number, even if it is only a contact number. Agencies are very unlikely to put you on their books unless they can phone you when work comes up. When calling to enquire about work, or answer advertisements, be clear and confident. Remember that your accent is totally unfamiliar to most Australians. Give your name clearly, introduce yourself and state why you are calling.

Your telephone manner can be vital, if you cannot make yourself understood, you will not get the job.

The Junior system – a question of age

Age is very important for most Australian jobs. Many young people leave school (some at 15) and go straight on to the jobs market. Rates of pay, related to age, are set out in some union pay awards. 'Junior' is often specified in job ads and means that the job will go to a young person and will be paid at the lower junior rate. Unless you are sure your talents are so dazzling that you can persuade the company to make an adult job of it, forget it.

The Interview

There are commonsense rules for interviews all over the world. . . be on time, be prepared, bring references and examples of your work. . . you know all this. Australian interviews differ from Irish ones though, in a number of ways, some quite startling. First, they are more casual. You will usually be interviewed by just one person who will be quite informal and probably use first names. You are unlikely to come under any demanding rapid-fire questioning, but you will not get into details about the job unless you make the opportunity. This casual attitude is good in many ways, as you get a chance to sell yourself, but do not get lulled into a cosy chat. Be more professional than the interviewer.

Dress quite smartly, but do not overdo it. Make as many openings as you can to talk about the job and your own experience. There will probably be more room to build on this and put it in a good light than there would be in Ireland. For one thing, overseas experience is difficult to check on and the employer will probably not be familiar with the comparative Irish scene. Make comparisons and contrasts with Ireland and demonstrate your suitability in terms of experience. Be confident and remember to speak clearly. Your accent and position as a new arrival may work against you. Try to show your familiarity with your area of work in Australia.

Be prepared for some hypocritical flattery. Your qualifications may be 'wonderful', your experience 'terrific', you may be 'just the person'. . . and never hear from them again. This is fairly common in Australia, one drawback of the more casual approach.

If you feel the interview has gone well, and you are not offered the job on the spot, it is no harm to pursue it by telephone. Call the next day, and even call again. The employer may have had some misgivings about taking on someone who isn't Australian. If you show your determination you could change his mind. Generally, you should be offered the job almost immediately, either that day or within a week. Employers do not have the same masses of applications to sift through that they do here, nor do they waste time.

People on working-holiday visas have some special problems at interviews. Remember that you are expected not to keep any job for more than three months. Always bring your passport in case employers or employment agencies want to check that you are actually allowed to work. Lying about being on a working-holiday, even if it is not found out on the spot, will muddy the water for Irish people who come to the same employer after you. If you like Australia though, and would like to settle there, do not hesitate to tell your potential employer at the interview. You may be able to apply for residency while on the job, or to return to it having gone through the processes back in Ireland.

Fair go

If you are offered part-time hours, or a few casual shifts, perhaps instead of the full-time work advertised, take it. It is common for an employer to try you out before committing the firm to employing you. The idea of a fair go, of giving everyone a fair opportunity to make the most of and get started, is an Australian tradition of which they are proud. You are getting a chance to prove yourself – use it. Lay into the work, get to know your workmates and your immediate superiors and learn on the job – fast. Chances are you will be working yourself into a full-time place. Of course, if you are absolutely useless, you will be given your marching orders without much hesitation.

Working-holidays

People on working-holiday visas are really limited to casual work. This means you should try areas of work which are likely to offer jobs on a temporary basis. Seasonal work is an obvious outlet – see the next section. Also likely are jobs in catering; hospital kitchens and factory canteens often employ people on this basis. Hospitality jobs in areas which do not have many tourists are not as likely, but you could try for waitressing, kitchen-hand and cashier jobs in restaurants, and cleaning, porter and bar service jobs in bars and hotels. Lounge boys and girls are not very common in Australia. Supermarket cashiers and shop assistants are rarely employed on a casual basis, unless at a particularly busy time of the year like Christmas. People with special skills, especially in word-processing and other office technology, are very likely to pick up temporary work from employment agencies. Receptionists with the ability to handle large switchboards are also likely to get short-term relief work, so too are legal secretaries and accounts' clerks.

Nurses would have no difficulty, either working through an agency or getting casual shifts by applying directly to hospitals. Nurse's aides and porters are sometimes sought by hospitals on a casual basis. Teachers may get some hours of 'supply' teaching (temporary replacement, or subbing). For public schools, this is usually organised by the State Department of Education. For private schools, you can apply directly. If you have a good qualification in Teaching English as a Foreign Language, private language schools are a possibility. Most would demand people with good experience. Both nurses and teachers must be registered with the relevant State department to be allowed work in public institutions.

All casual work will be offered on the basis of experience and qualifications. Waitress, bar and secretarial work will not go to (or be kept by) people who do not come up to scratch with speed and efficiency. People who assume they can walk into a job on the basis of their dynamic personality alone will find themselves severely tested.

Seasonal work – Agriculture and Hospitality

Seasonal work is mostly available in agriculture and hospitality. (Hospitality is the Australian term for tourist and other, similar, service industries – casino, hotel, restaurant and bar work, couriers and tourist guides.) Seasonal work is rarely well-paid. In agriculture, for example, it usually depends on how much you do. Nevertheless, it may be useful for those on working-holiday visas as it is almost always casual work, either temporary or part-time.

Agriculture
Agricultural jobs may be found in fruit-picking, vegetable and grain harvesting and in processing and packing on farms and wineries. Your local branch of the Commonwealth Employment Service should be able to tell you the dates of the various seasons. Possible sources of this kind of work include CES notice boards, newspaper ads and, if you are in the right area, local newspapers. It is also worthwhile calling in to farmers and asking. Here, the local shop or hotel may be able to help, but be sure of how far away the farm is. Distances between them can be huge. When working, on-site accommodation or camping is standard.

This is a brief list of some likely areas for fruit, grape and vegetable picking, with approximate seasons:

Tasmania; apples, March–May, potatoes, February–April:

South Australia (Barossa Valley); grapes, February–April:

Queensland (Bundaberg area); tropical fruit, January–April, (Kingaroy area) peanuts, March–May, (Atherton tableland) potatoes and vegetables, something going on all year round:

Western Australia (Kalamunda, Armadale, Kelmscott and other suburban areas); fruit, citrus, September–October; fruit, stone, June–August; (Donnybrook area); apples, March–May:

Victoria (Murray River area); grapes and soft fruit, February–April.

Jackaroos and Jillaroos are the Australian versions of cowboys and cowgirls or station hands. Beware of advertisements in country newspapers, and in some of the more countrified city ones, for jobs like these. They require people with the experience, knowledge of the bush and survival skills to get through tough outback life, often on stations that are very remote. Unless you are another Crocodile Dundee, forget it.

Hospitality
Hospitality jobs in tourist resorts may be quite easy to pick

up if you are about in the right season. Write to the big hotels in the resorts, use the CES and employment agencies. Even call in, if you are in the area. Do not make the journey 'on spec', unless you want to see the place anyway.

Among the areas you might try are:

Queensland: all coastal towns and resort islands have a fast- changing population of casual staff in hotels, bars and restaurants. Try resort islands like Great Keppel, Fitzroy and Green. The more expensive 'exclusive' places will want top-class staff. For really casual work, try Magnetic Island.

NSW and Victoria: Ski resorts in the Snowy Mountains and the Victorian Alps respectively may provide some opportunities. Among the possibilities are Mt Buller, Mt Baw Baw, Falls Creek (Victoria) and Thredbo, Perisher and Smiggin Holes (NSW). The season is very short, July to September, and the resorts are expensive if you do not have work. Ski resort jobs in New Zealand are said to be better and easier to find.

Northern Territory: Yulara, the resort for Ayers Rock, has several upmarket hotels with casual work opportunities. Guide work (showing people around the resort and handling tourist queries) may also be available, especially if you are pretty. Peak season is June to August.

There are many other popular resort areas. Use your head. Anywhere that is a popular destination for tourists, will need people to serve them.

Pay and Conditions

Job categories, the award system

Payment and conditions of work in Australia depend on job category. This will be mentioned in the advertisement or stipulated by the employer. There are four main categories of job: casual, temporary, part-time and full-time (permanent).

Almost all rates of pay in these categories are based on an award system. This means the minimum rate of pay and conditions agreed between the appropriate union or trade association and employers in Federal or State Industrial tribunals. Award rates and conditions will vary according to job category.

Casual work is usually given an hourly rate of pay and no sick pay, holiday, maternity, pension or any other benefits, depending on the award for the job in question. No notice period is usually necessary on either side. There are exceptions, however, so ask. Nearly all seasonal work, agency jobs (both secretarial and nursing), bar and restaurant work and supply teaching will be on a casual basis. Most people on working-holiday visas or newly arrived in the country will have this type of job, at least initially. Temporary and part-time jobs are also usually paid on a casual basis, though some part-time jobs are permanent.

Full-time work will have all the benefits and conditions of a salaried job, if it is permanent. If so, the employer may pay above award rates in recognition of special skills, qualifications or years of experience. Sometimes unions and management will have negotiated payment above the official minimum award in a particular company. It is possible to begin work on a full-time basis, and be paid at casual rates, for an initial trial period. After this (usually three months), you and the employer may sign a contract and you will become permanent. Some people work in full-time jobs for years and are paid a casual rate. Try to avoid this, you have little security and may miss out on entitlement to paid annual leave, sick benefit, long-service leave and all the other excellent conditions of the Australian work place.

A general rule is to accept casual rates if you are looking for short-term work, on a working-holiday visa or starting off in a job. If you intend to stick around and want a career, see your employer about becoming permanent after three months. Some companies and agencies, often in less skilled areas, with more casual staff who are not heavily unionised, (for example : office cleaning, kitchen work) will pay below award rates. There is little you can do about this other than find out what the official award is and find another job which pays it. You will get this information from the union or professional association in your field.

Pay

Pay will vary with job category, qualifications, experience, work conditions and perks, agency fees (if any) and, of course, how closely your employer sticks to that all-important pay award. Many awards contain loading for night and weekend work, and other allowances for working in remote areas. For up-to-date figures on your field, check the newspaper ads in the Embassy library in Dublin.

Some examples of casual rates follow.

Waiter/waitress: $5.25 an hour award minimum, but can be paid up to $9 above award, with extra for speed and efficiency. There are few tips. Awards are loaded for weekends and so on.

Secretary/typist: $7 an hour minimum, but can go up to $20 and more, depending on speed and experience.

Bank clerk/accounts clerk/cashier: Anything from $7 an hour to $12, it varies a lot with agencies.

Barman/barmaid: $10 minimum an hour, will increase with efficiency and experience.

Journalist: Casual award rate on a metropolitan paper is a B- grading, equivalent to about $130 a shift, plus holiday pay.

Most unskilled jobs (kitchen-hand, porter, shop assistant) will be paid upwards of $4 an hour.

Nurse: Rates vary a lot, with extra pay for qualifications, experience and areas of work (maternity, intensive-care unit and so on). There is also loading for weekends and work after 6.00 pm. A shift of night duty (10 pm to 8.00 am) may earn $190. Many hospitals operate a pool system, so there is opportunity for part-time work, job-sharing and overtime, as well as working a standard five-day week. Generally, pay is excellent. Agencies usually charge about 6% of gross pay.

Teacher: Hourly supply teaching and private language school rates are about $20. This varies a lot with qualifications and experience.

Men and women in the work-place
The principle of equal pay for equal work was established by the Commonwealth Arbitration Commission in 1969. Both men and women can apply for all jobs provided they are suitably qualified and are entitled to equal pay, unless sex is stipulated in the advertisement. This can and does happen, if it is felt only one sex or the other can do the job. It is also sometimes necessary to read between the lines. 'Attractive

well-presented receptionist required', is unlikely to go to a strapping Kerry Buck.

Women's average weekly earnings still lag behind those of men, even though over 40% of the labour force is female. This is because they are more often in temporary or part-time jobs and paid casual rates. Average weekly earnings for women in 1985 were $334.40, men $404.50. The average working couple earns $728 gross a week. The average weekly household income, taking into account non-working spouses is $451.48. Married women account for about 58% of the female labour force.

7 The System... Banking, Tax, Health and the Law

This can be no more than an introduction to a whole new world. While Australia and Ireland run on the same basic principles about the rule of law, health care and liberal parliamentary democracy, many of the details are different. Migrants may use the special advisory services for migrants, there are also citizens' advice bureaux in some cities and public libraries carry a good deal of information about your rights and obligations. The best source, of course, for day-to-day information is the advice of friends, sponsors, workmates and relations.

One pleasant feature of life in Australia is that government, state and semi-state bodies are happy to tell you all they can. Most have a wide range of brochures and leaflets covering all aspects of their services and will cheerfully fill in any gaps if you telephone them. It would be tempting to make comparisons with our own country.

Banking

One of your first concerns on arrival, or even before going to Australia will be to open a bank account. The major Australian banks include Westpac, the Commonwealth Bank, the State Bank of Victoria, the State Bank of South Australia, the Rural & Industries Bank of Western Australia and the Australia and New Zealand Bank (ANZ).

For size and convenience, it is better to stick to Westpac, the Commonwealth or ANZ, and preferably one of the first two. They both have a huge number of hole-in-the-wall cash machines scattered across Australia. Having spent years competing with each other with these machines, they decided in 1987 to make their machines reciprocal. You can now use your Westpac card in the Commonwealth machines and vice versa.

If you intend living or staying in London before you head off for Australia, you can open an account before you go. Even if you are not going to London, it is worth getting in touch with the banks and availing of their advice. The Commonwealth for example, publishes in-depth analyses of the cost of living in each State, which are comprehensive and usually up-to-date. It also has all sorts of other useful literature. See the Useful Addresses section.

Since 1966, the Australian currency has been the Australian dollar, of 100 cents. There are notes of 100, 50, 20, 10, 5 and 2 dollars and coins of 1 dollar, 50 cents, 20 cents, 10 cents, 5 cents, 2 cents and 1 cent. In December 1987, an Australian dollar was worth 45 Irish pence. While this varies, the usual rule of thumb is to multiply or divide by two to convert currencies.

On arrival in Australia, you will probably have a substantial amount of money to open your new account. Use this to strike a good bargain with the bank. All the banks compete with packages of accounts, cheque books, cash-machine cards, free banking in certain areas and so on. Collect the brochures from several banks and find the package that suits you best.

Plastic Cards

The same two major credit cards operate in Australia as in Ireland; Mastercard (Commonwealth and Westpac) and Visa (State Bank of Victoria and Rural & Industries). Unlike Mastercard in Ireland, there is no interest-free period on goods bought, so it is to your advantage to clear accounts quickly. There is also Bankcard, issued by the major banks, which does allow an interest-free period, but cannot be used outside the country.

Be careful when opening your account that you ask for a statement at intervals that suit you. If you do not, they will send you a snake of computer paper once a year, on which most of the transactions are so long ago that there is little hope of correcting any errors.

Whatever type of account you open, make sure that you get a card for the cash machine with it. While banking hours are sensibly longer than in Ireland, it is still handy to be able to get cash day and night. Many shops also have terminals that allow you to have purchases debited from your account instead of paying in cash. Once you have a card, you can do virtually all your banking without ever setting foot in a bank building.

It is usually wise to wait until you have a job before looking for a Mastercard or Visa card. The banks are not terribly fussy about them, but they like you to have some sort of regular income. Once you get a credit card, it can be used to address all your accounts with that bank and to swap money between them, to get a balance and to clear credit-card bills.

Australian banks do not issue cheque guarantee cards (banker's cards), which limits the usefulness of your cheque book. Therefore, it is useful to have a credit card even if you have no need of the credit element. Your credit card can be used for everything from mail-order shopping to dial-an-erotic-phone-call services.

It is your choice as to how you bring your money with you, but it is worth having at least some cash to get by until you can cash your travellers' cheques or lodge your bank draft.

One word of warning is needed. Interest rates are high in Australia and credit is easy come by. Banks blare their free and easy approach to credit in lurid day-glo signs in the window. They will allow you to borrow large sums or run them up on your credit card. The only snag is that they want it all back – plus a hefty interest bill. Be careful with credit. There is an extensive credit-reference computer system in operation and one bad debt can make life very hard for you afterwards.

Lastly, if you are heading off to the wilds on holiday, it is worth opening an old-fashioned pass-book account with Westpac or the Commonwealth. Fancy credit cards and cash-machine cards are of no use in a town with no bank, as the authors discovered to their cost in Strahan, Tasmania and on Magnetic Island, Queensland. Even where there is no bank, a local shop or post office will often act as agent for pass-book accounts.

Health

Medicare
Australia has had a good universal health-care service, Medicare, since 1984. It is partly financed by a 1.25% levy on all salaries. People earning under $6,698 a year, pensioners, war veterans and widows and armed forces members are exempt from the levy. Nor does it apply to income over $70,000 dollars a year. This still means that most Irish people working in

Australia, whether migrants or working-holiday visitors, will be paying the levy. They must, however, have permission to stay in Australia for over six months to qualify for a Medicare card.

There are Medicare offices in most towns and suburbs. You just visit the office, fill in a form and the card arrives within a week or two. If you need treatment before the card arrives, you can delay payment until the card arrives or get your Medicare number from Medicare and use the number without the card.

Medicare covers 85% of the schedule fee for each visit to the doctor. The schedule fee is what Medicare thinks the visit should cost. Beware of doctors who charge more. The doctor may 'bulk-bill' Medicare, in which case you pay nothing, or, if you pay him, you get back 85% of what you have paid across the counter at a Medicare office, no hassle, no fuss. Just keep the receipt.

Medicare covers specialist consultations as long as you have been referred by your doctor and also covers eye tests, but no drugs or glasses. It covers public-ward hospital accommodation and treatment by the hospital's own doctors.

Unfortunately, Medicare is under attack, both from a government bent on saving money and from certain sections of the medical world. It is very difficult to have eye surgery in New South Wales on Medicare, for example, as many eye surgeons there will not co-operate with Medicare. As the service is pruned, waiting lists grow.

Private health cover
There is a flourishing scene in private health insurance in Australia. Most of the schemes are similar to the VHI in this country, with levels of treatment cover depending on contributions. These schemes were once a tax-avoiding ploy in that companies paid the contributions for their workers, but the government has clamped down on this by taxing the health contributions as fringe benefits.

Medical costs can be substantial in Australia, so it is wise to seek private cover if you are not under Medicare. In each State there is a private health organisation with a transfer arrangement with the VHI. Ask the VHI about the one in the State you intend to arrive in. The advantages of such a transfer is that there is no break in your cover and you can claim benefit from the beginning. If you are not a member of the VHI, you will have to start from scratch with a private scheme and will have to pay for some time before you get benefits. For expensive elective services, such as orthodontic work, this can be a matter of years.

Many Australians covered by Medicare decide to top up their cover with a private fund. This allows them a choice of doctor in hospital, benefit for glasses and other items not covered by Medicare. The popular wisdom is that a healthy young person can afford to rely on Medicare only, although this may change if there are further cutbacks.

Ambulances

Ambulances in Australia charge fees – like very expensive taxis. While they will not present the bill at the scene of the accident, it will certainly arrive if you need to use an ambulance. Some classes of private cover will pay for your ambulance. Medicare will not. You can insure against a large ambulance bill (they can run to hundreds of dollars) or, in Western Australia, make a $15 donation to the ambulance service. This entitles you to a free ride.

Short-term visitors can insure before they leave home (ask your travel agent) or they can join one of the special short-term schemes operated by the private funds. Unlike the long-term schemes, these will allow instant benefit.

You need have few worries about the standard of care in Australia. By and large it is excellent. In some areas, Australian doctors are at the forefront of world research and innovation. Of course, it is still wise to get the advice of a friend, workmate or relative about suitable doctors in your area.

Medicare does not cover dental treatment, and dental care does not come cheap in Australia. Does it anywhere? Visitors should have their teeth hammered into shape before they leave Ireland. Those staying longer may want private cover especially for this.

Tax

Taxation in Australia is a complicated business. Federal, State and local governments all want their slice of your little cake. In the case of the latter two, the stamp duties, payroll tax, motor tax, land tax and service charges are levied by State and local government, the systems and amounts vary from State to State and from town to town within a State. By and large, they will come to you.

The Federal Government hits you with income tax, capital gains tax, fringe benefits tax, customs and excise, departure tax and sales tax. As mentioned, government departments and offices will be happy to provide you with explanatory leaflets and information.

Watch out for the departure tax of $20. Everyone leaving Australia must pay it. Remember to keep the money at the end of your stay or your merry gallop through the airport on the way back to the oul' sod will be brought to an unsympathetic halt.

Tax advice

Income-tax advisers (or IT 'professionals' as they call themselves) proliferate in Australia. Have one recommended to you and bring your questions to them having swotted up on the leaflets. The advisers' fees may be claimed against your tax.

You may well have to call on one, as income tax in Australia can be a bit of a minefield. All residents of Australia must pay tax on their income from inside and outside Australia. Those staying for less than six months do not qualify as residents for tax purposes. They, and other non-residents, pay 30% tax on earnings up to $19,500 and the same rate as residents above that.

Income tax in Australia is paid in two stages. On starting a job, you fill out a form. Remember to keep a copy. It is illegal to have two of these tax declarations in force at the same time. Your employer will then deduct tax from your pay packet each week. The second stage comes at the end of the tax year on 30 June. Within two months of that date, you must fill a tax return (available, with instructions, from any post office) and send it in. The fact that the Federal Treasurer failed to lodge a return for several months after the deadline will not cut much ice with the authorities if you follow his example.

Your tax return must have details of your income from all sources and full information for any claims you want to make for expenses such as union membership or work clothes. You prove your weekly earnings and the tax paid on them, by producing 'group certificates'. Your employer is obliged to give you one of these. Demand it when you leave a job.

Your tax return is assessed by the authorities and you are either given a rebate, or woe of woes, asked for more tax. Generally, your PAYE payments will cover your tax bill unless you have substantial other earnings.

The PAYE tax rates for individuals in force since 1 July 1987 are as follows.

Dollars	Tax
$5,100 and under	nil
$5,101 to $12,600	24%
$12,601 to $19,500	29%
$19,501 to $35,000	40%
$35,001 and over	49%

All pay packets are lightened by 1.25%, before tax, to pay for Medicare. If you do not get a Medicare card, when the time comes to lodge a tax return ask for your Medicare levy back.

Taxation of businesses, partnerships and companies is complex and requires professional advice. When there are large sums involved, with leading businessmen and professionals, Australians are resourceful in finding ways around the tax system. The present government is doing its best to plug these loopholes and the situation changes rapidly.

The Law

The legal system is modelled, as is ours, on that of the United Kingdom. It grew with the colonies from a system of military courts. Civil courts and trial by jury were introduced in the first half of the last century. In line with the colonial status of Australia at the time, British common law was applied, as were some British statutes. The High Court of Australia was established in 1900. There is also a complete court system in each State, from magistrates' courts up to the State supreme court. The State systems are the courts of general jurisdiction, with powers to decide Federal as well as State matters unless some Federal court has exclusive jurisdiction in the area.

The links with the British legal system remain strong. It is only very recently, for example, that the practice of appealing to the Privy Council in London as an ultimate authority was discontinued. That much said, Australia has been far more sensible than this country in overhauling ancient laws inherited from Britain. Where we often hear of people being charged under some primitive British law, the Australians have replaced much of the archaic law with State and Federal law more applicable to the modern world.

Special courts

As well as the mainstream civil and criminal courts, there are small claims courts and tribunals in Queensland, Victoria, New South Wales and Western Australia. These hear complaints by consumers against traders with a simplified legal format and low costs. Australian consumer law is strong and there is no need to accept shoddy goods or services. In South Australia, the Australian Capital Territory and, more recently, in Queensland lower courts have been given special jurisdiction to hear small claims.

Other courts, like the Industrial division of the Federal Court and the Conciliation and Arbitration Commission deal with industrial disputes and pay claims. There is also an ombudsman in each State and at Federal level. Their main function is to investigate complaints from the public about government bodies. They are independent of politicians and can bring their findings directly to Parliament if they wish.

Criminal law varies from State to State, but five principles are common to each system:

★ A person is presumed innocent until proved guilty.
★ The prosecution must prove criminal charges and it is not the responsibility of the accused to disprove them.
★ Accused or suspected people are not obliged to make any statement to the police.
★ If an accused is tried and found not guilty, he or she cannot be charged with another offence where the same facts are used.
★ The prosecution must demonstrate an intent to break the law.

Legal abortion is available in some States. Divorce is freely available Australia-wide. One facet of Australian law is worth noting. *De facto* marriage, (known in Ireland as 'living in sin') is recognised as marriage for some tax, immigration and other procedures.

Police
The blunt end of the law is the Federal and State police forces. All are armed. You would be well advised not to come under the attention of either.

There are variations, but police powers are generally as follows.

★ They can make arrests only on reasonable grounds for believing the suspect is guilty (these grounds may be tested in court), on warrant, or without a warrant under the same conditions as a citizen may make an arrest (generally reasonable suspicion that someone has committed, or is about to commit a felony).

★ If a person is not legally arrested, he has no obligation to obey the instructions of a policeman.

★ The police cannot detain a person for questioning. An arrested person must be brought before a magistrate as soon as possible.

★ The police have the right to enter and search premises for reasons which vary a great deal from State to State.

★ Individual rights are strongly protected in relation to police questioning. Generally, no suspect is required to answer questions or to provide their name and address. As here, a large proportion of convictions stem from confessions made to police during questioning.

Driving
The main area in which Australian law will impinge on the average law-abiding Irish visitor or migrant is in relation to driving. Bring an international driving licence with you, as well as your Irish one. International licences are available from the Automobile Association for a small fee. If on a working-holiday, delay getting the licence until shortly before you leave, as it is valid for only one year from date of issue. You are entitled to drive on your Irish licence but car-hire companies often prefer to see your handsome Irish mug on the licence to ensure it is actually yours.

If you are staying for some time, you will need an Australian licence – issued by the States. To get one, produce your Irish licence at the local department of transport, have an eye test and a highway code test and away you go – as long as your Irish licence has no endorsements on it. Remember to carry your licence when you drive. In some States it is an offence not to be able to produce it on the spot.

The highway code varies from State to State, as do traffic rules. They drive on the left as we do, but there are some variations. There is a 'give way to the right' rule, which means that if you are driving and see a car emerging from a road to the right you must give way to it. Usually, minor roads are signposted to show who has right of way. But in some areas, like rural Queensland and some residential areas, you must be very careful. In Victoria, there is an extra twist to this rule. if two cars approaching each other turn into the same street, the one turning right has priority. At some intersections in Melbourne (clearly marked) cars intending to turn right must pull in to the left-hand side of the road. Try to follow someone else's lead and watch out for the trams. It can be very hard to get off a freeway if you miss a turn, so check out your route in your city street guide before you start. Many Australians keep the street guide in the car.

Road law

Australia is metric. That includes speed limits and distance signs. The 110 sign is not an invitation to try for the old-fashioned ton. The general speed limit in urban areas is 60 kilometres per hour. On the open road, it ranges from 100 to 110 kph. There is no general speed limit on the open road in the Northern Territory.

The police are fond of setting speed traps and collect large sums of money this way. Part of the reason is the determined nationwide campaign to get the level of death on the roads reduced. Even in the open country police sometimes use spotter planes to catch speeding motorists by timing them between two set marks. Some traffic lights are neatly wired up with beams to detect those who break the lights and with cameras to snap them in the act. Be careful.

Far more serious is driving under the influence of drink, drugs or both. Random breath testing is widespread. Especially at holiday periods and Christmas, the police work their way through hundreds of motorists. They sometimes even stake out parties and test everyone who leaves. Drunk driving, or DD, is seen as a social menace and in some areas the names of all those convicted are published in the local newspapers. The penalties are severe and 'the limit' is lower than in Ireland.

Drugs
Whether in a car or not, the use and possession of illegal recreational drugs can also attract severe penalties. Australia has a marvellous climate for growing cannabis and it is widely used, but the penalties for being caught in possession of it vary widely. New South Wales and Victoria are comparatively lenient on those convicted of having small amounts of it, while in Queensland the punishments are draconian. Penalties for dealing in cannabis and for the abuse of hard drugs are uniformly severe.

Welfare and Social Security

There are a wide range of social security and welfare benefits available. Working-holiday and other short-term visitors are not entitled to them. Beware of Commonwealth Employment Service desk officials who try to persuade you that the border with Northern Ireland is really rather academic and that you are entitled to dole like a British citizen. The system can be abused, but fraud is often detected and the penalties are harsh. There is no social standing in being called a 'dole bludger'.

The benefits include the following; Unemployment Benefit, Sickness Benefit, Disability Pension, Service Pension, Double Orphan's Pension, Handicapped Child's Allowance, Family Income Supplement, Family Allowance, Rehabilitation Allowance, Sheltered Employment Allowance, Supporting Parent's Benefit, Widow's Pension, Spouse Carer's Pension, Wife's Pension, Age Pension and Invalid Pension.

If you believe that you qualify for any of these benefits, pensions or allowances get in touch with your local Department of Social Security office or with the department at: Juliana House, Bowes Street, Phillip, Australian Capital Territory 2606, Phone (0602) 891 444.

Immigration

Irish people who are admitted to Australia as migrants are given permanent residence visas. After two years, they may apply for Australian citizenship. Irish people who do so do not forefeit their Irish citizenship. Those who do not take up Australian citizenship will need a resident return visa to get back into the country after trips abroad. At present, this resident return visa, valid for three years, is given out with migrant visas. If you do not take up citizenship within this time, remember to get a resident return visa before leaving Australia.

Change of status

People temporarily in Australia may apply for permanent residence under a number of conditions. Among these are: if they have been given asylum by Australia, or are the spouse, child or aged parent of an Australian citizen or permanent resident, or are authorised to work in Australia and are not a student or diplomat.

Anyone making such an application, however, must meet the same criteria as would be applied in their home embassies. These include the points test, recognition of qualifications and health and character requirements. There are no free points for being on the spot.

8 Settling In

Making Friends

Australian cities may *look* similar to those in Ireland and Europe, Australian people may seem similar to Irish people – but they are not. All sorts of differences exist between those in the Southern Hemisphere and we of the cold North, and the longer you stay the more these become apparent. People use different language, spend their spare time doing different things, relate to each other differently, and may have a different perspective on their place in the affairs of the globe. To make the most of your time in Australia, or to make a happy transfer to living there permanently, you must be open-minded, unprejudiced and ready to learn.

We are all guilty of stereotypes – how many friends to whom you mentioned going to Australia responded with 'G'day Mate' and spoke of beer-drinking Ozzies, hats with corks, Kangaroos, Crocodile Dundee and surfboards? Of course these are features of Australia, even if some are kept going by the tourist trade. The country is so vast, and inhabited by people of so many different races, ethnic origins, interests and lifestyles that the only generalisation you can safely make is about its infinite variety. Super-cliché number one is 'It's a big country . . .' You will hear it again and again, even find yourself saying it.

Do not keep making comparisons, favourable or otherwise, with the 'old country'. Tell people about it if they are interested. Comments on differences are likely to be misinterpreted, complaints are treated unsympathetically. The logic is, you *chose* to come to Australia. Sounds reasonable enough.

Some Australians will be dying to tell you their latest Irish jokes. While having a sense of humour and ability to laugh at yourself is an essential for Australian life, so too is plain speaking. Do not reinforce cultural stereotypes. Defend yourself and your country on your own terms. The convicts and bush-rangers, navvies and skivvies, bigots and bishops who contributed to Australian life in earlier times and gave many Australians their image of the Irish are being replaced all the time, particularly, in these times of recession, by trained, professional young people. You, whatever your aims, will have a part to play in making the Irish image multi-faceted and up to date.

Be prepared for endless questions from friends and work-mates as to why you have come. People are genuinely curious about you and your motivation. While money and having a reasonable standard of living are obviously important, try to let people know you are interested in and appreciate their country. The answer 'To make lots of money, drink beer and lie in the sun' sounds pretty pathetic. On the same note try not to knock the oul' sod too much. Australians are patriotic people and love their country – with reason. Scathing and endless criticism of your own land may make them uncomfortable.

Myth of the philistine Aussie
Of course there are Australians to whom the height of man's achievements is the invention of beer, whose idea of getting dressed up is to drag a singlet over their beer-guts and who would sooner eat a book than read one. There are plenty of Irish people of whom the same things are true. In both cases, they are the exceptions.

The idea that all Australians are beer-swilling louts, that Australian men's conception of foreplay consists of the words 'brace yerself Sheila', that all things Australian are crude imitations of those of Europe is utter rubbish. If you entertain any suspicion that it is true, better leave it behind.

The myth of the philistine Aussie has its origins in British superciliousness and snobbery. It comes from the same place as the idea that all Irish people are 'fearfully Celtic', all writers, drinkers and fighters, who run around with a shillelagh in one hand, a rosary in the other and a bottle of whiskey tucked under an elbow.

Don't regard Australian wine as alcoholic lemonade. If you want cheap wine, you can buy it far cheaper than in Ireland, but if you pay a little more and take some interest in it, you can enjoy first-class wine from great Australian wineries. The same holds good for Australian art, music, literature and culture of all sorts. Keep an open mind, put in a little effort and you will be richly rewarded.

One sure way to lose Australian friends, or to avoid making

any, is to treat everything Australian as second-rate and 'colonial' – or to join with the 'whingeing poms' who do so.

The Media

Despite having a small population spread over a massive area, or perhaps because of it, Australia is a media-mad society. The media of mass communication have an enormous impact on the life of the average Australian and in turn, these media are the basis of a massive, competitive industry.

At the beginning of 1985 there were 538 newspapers, over 1,400 magazines, 320 radio stations and 146 television stations in Australia, as well as some 650 cinemas. It has been estimated that 98% of Australian homes have a television and that 99% have a radio. In 1984, advertisers spent nearly $3,000 million on advertising in the mass media.

You will probably spend much of your free time on one or more of the products of the communications' industry, collapsing in front of the television after a hard day at work, scanning the newspaper for jobs and news of home (do not hold your breath waiting for Irish news). So what is out there?

Newspapers
You will never run short of a newspaper in Australia. There is a wealth of them, from *The Sydney Morning Herald* and *The Age*, two of the great newspapers of the world, to *The Cootamundra Herald*, which has a circulation of about 2,000. Because of the huge distances between cities, there is only one general news national paper, *The Australian*. The pattern, for the rest, is one or two morning papers in a major city, depending on its size, with one or two evenings and a couple of weeklies. You will be relying on the quality morning paper in each city for job and accommodation advertising. These are: *The Age*, Melbourne; *The Courier-Mail*, Brisbane; *The Sydney Morning Herald*; *The West Australian*, Perth; *The Canberra Times*; *The Advertiser*, Adelaide; *The Mercury*, Hobart; and *The Northern Territory News*, Darwin.

National weeklies include the beautifully designed *Times on Sunday* and the unusually named bi-weekly *Truth*, which specialises in UFO stories. By and large, Australian newspapers are bright, snappy and excellent value for money.

The papers, and the media generally, will help you get into

the swing of life in Australia, getting you clued in on the issues of the day and demonstrating the priorities of Australian life. One of the first things you will notice is the concentration on news of the region, south-east Asia. Events that barely rate a mention in Ireland will get careful attention if they impinge on Australia or her neighbours. While there is a special interest in Britain, do not expect detailed news on Ireland. Bombs and elections are about the extent of coverage, even in the quality papers. Irish newspapers too are very hard to get. Try the newspaper reading room of your State library.

Television

The average Australian spends about 20 hours a week in front of the tube. You would be forgiven for wondering why at times. The TV system, like that in Britain, has two elements, the public ABC (and SBS), and the private commercial stations licensed by the Federal Governement.

It is not economic to distribute TV signals nation-wide as RTE does, so the stations vary from area to area. The major cities, or most of them, have three commercial stations (Channels 7, 9 and 10) as well as the ABC (Channel 2) and SBS, which transmits special-interest programmes for linguistic and other minorities.

The ABC strives to follow the best traditions of public service broadcasting, as exemplified by the mother of such broadcasting, the BBC. It is usually your best bet for quality programmes and mercifully carries no ads. On the other hand, it captures only about 15% of the national audience. Its finances are at the mercy of politicians and it does not get the resources needed to fulfil all its potential.

Commercial TV is similar to its British equivalents, except that controls on advertising and programme quality appear to be much more relaxed. Its staples are soap operas, game shows and news, with films and mini-series. There is an awful lot of advertising, noticeably more than in Ireland and Britain, and enough to irritate most people to distraction. Worse still is the system by which the audience ratings are calculated and ad prices set. There are 'ratings periods' during which the stations hit you with their very best product, all at the same time, and for a short period. Between 'ratings periods', they can pump out any old garbage they like, and often do.

Among the redeeming features is the fact that these stations have a lot of money to spend on covering news and sporting events. They zip off in helicopters to get the story, and the pictures, in situations where RTE might not spend the money. One other plus is that they run late at night, and some of them all night.

But this counted for little with a well known journalist who said, on going back to Sydney after 14 years away: 'If you have seen American television and can imagine it without its redeeming features, then Australian TV is even worse than that.'

Radio

As in television, there are public-service and commercial stations. In the cities you will have plenty to choose from. ABC Radio National does very good news and current affairs shows and also broadcasts the proceedings of Parliament, which are well worth a listen every now and again. On the commercial stations, the choice is yours, from classical music to talk-back shows to the usual pop music interspersed with pseudo-American psychobabble, it is all there. Although some Irish radio shows use audience phone-ins, none has taken it to the lengths of Australian talk-back radio. Here the public makes the show, a constant stream of callers bounce their ideas off the host. It can be good fun and an introduction to the thinking of ordinary Australians, or at least the ones who call radio shows. Some papers list only TV shows, so you may have to rely on weekly supplements of radio listings to find out what is on.

Magazines

This is an area of wide, almost bewildering, choice. Top of the heap is *Australian Women's Weekly* (published monthly, so figure that one out), which sells over a million copies. There are all sorts of specialist magazines, but unfortunately no excellent current affairs one. *The Bulletin* is the nearest thing. You can also buy some of your old favourites from home, sent out surface and months out of date. *Hot Press* and *Private Eye* are both sold in this way.

Getting through – phone and post

Australian Postal and Telecommunications services are

under the Federal control of the Department of Communications. They are both highly efficient and service-conscious organisations – perhaps because they are statutory authorities whose charters require them to meet their annual operating expenditures and at least 50% of capital expenditure from internal revenue.

Telecom

The telephone service provides a huge range of facilities as well as mere phones. Public telephone services definitely fall short of their high-tech communications facilities, including those available to the private user. Home telephones are often pushbutton models, with memory and recall functions. Their costs and installation are dealt with under Services. Public telephones are being slowly updated and numbers increased. There are three types of payphones, red, grey/green and gold.

Red payphones are most often found in local shops, shopping centres and bars. They take thirty cents – one 20 cent coin and a ten. These are being replaced, as they can only be used for local calls, and you may still find some which cost only 20 cents. Red phones often have no booths or hoods and tend to be in noisy places.

Grey/green payphones are the second most common type. These provide local and STD calls (long-distance within the country stands for Subscriber Trunk Dialling). Some have been updated to provide ISD (International Subscriber Dialling) and will take $1 coins. Most only take 50 and 20 cent coins. They are fitted with a red warning light which flashes when your time is almost up, so you can insert more money – if you have it to hand – or have time to say goodbye. If you complete your call before the money is used up, unused coins are returned. If you are making a long-distance call, it is useful to insert a heap of coins at the beginning which can then drop automatically, rather than waste precious seconds fumbling for change. This type of phone is most often to be found in post offices and on the street, especially in the suburbs. Watch out for their strange doors which always seem to fold the wrong way.

Gold payphones. The most up-to-date of the public telephone service, these are similar to the yellow electronic ones available here. A digital display tells you how much money you have left and flashes when your time is running out. A follow-on button can be used to dial another call, using remaining cash in the machine. If you hang up you only get the unused coins. They take all silver and $1 coins. All types of calls may be made; local, STD and ISD. These are the quietest and best value for international calls. They are usually to be found in secure, salubrious places like airports, hotel foyers, bars and some shops. If they are in a phonebox, a sticker to that effect will be on the door.

The code for dialling Ireland from Australia is international code (0011), plus the country code (Ireland = 353), plus the area code without the 0 used in Ireland (Dublin = 1), plus your number. If you want to call home on Christmas Day, book your call. Everyone has the same idea and an international line is hard to get. The emergency number, for fire, police or ambulance, is 000. Rates for ISD and STD calls vary with time of day, as here. All STD and ISD calls are cheaper at night and weekends, in other words, outside business hours. Special offers are sometimes advertised – look for super-special low-rates for the early hours of Sunday morning.

For those interested in statistics, 70% of outgoing overseas calls are handled automatically. International Subscriber Dialling is available to about 160 destinations. Telephone services are available to 230 overseas destinations. The Overseas Telecommunications Commission is responsible for these services, and all public telecommunications between Australia and other countries. You are billed through Telecom. OTC also provides facsimile, leased circuit, audio broadcast, electronic mail and data transmission services. If you want to send information or simply a birthday telegram from Australia there is a variety of ways. Especially personal is the 'imagegram' service whereby for about $12 your own drawing or message can be delivered by courier to the address in Ireland the same day. Heaps of glossy information leaflets about these services are available at post offices. Find out about them – they can work out cheaper than letters, telephone calls or old fashioned telegrams if you need something in a hurry.

Australia Post

The postal service is a very go-ahead consumer-conscious organisation. As well as providing stamps and mail delivery, they sell aerograms and pre-stamped envelopes and a variety of boxes and poster tubes (post packs). Cheap, lightweight and sturdy, these are ideal for sending presents or excess baggage home.

Postage for a letter within Australia is 37 cents at time of writing. Airmail postal charges are quite high – at present an aerogram costs 53 cents, a postcard 63 cents and a letter (20gm) $1. It takes about seven days for a letter to get from Ireland, though this can vary considerably from an amazing three days to over two weeks. If you are in no rush, surface mail (about 12 weeks) or surface airlift (about six weeks) are better value for parcels.

Post offices are generally open from 9 am–5 pm Monday to Friday. Some General Post Offices (GPOs) also open on Saturday morning. Stamps can sometimes be bought from local newsagents or suburban delis – they will have a sign to that effect. Australia Post is justifiably proud of its stamps – colourful and beautifully printed, they are a collector's dream. You can buy first-day covers and all sorts of special packages at any post office.

Other services include mail-holding, Poste Restante and redirection of mail. All GPOs have Poste Restante counters, a free service which will hold mail for you for one month if you have no address of your own. Make sure the name and surname are printed clearly, Irish names can give trouble, and those beginning with O' may be filed under that letter or the one following. To collect mail you need identification and if you are collecting on behalf of another person you need both that person's ID and a signed letter authorising you to do so. If you are changing address, you can arrange re-direction of mail. Go to your local post office, fill out a form, pay $3.50, have identification (and your new address!) with you. This service lasts a month and can be renewed – with payment of another fee, as you wish.

Australia Post is a massive organisation, employing nearly 33,000 people full-time to handle about 11 million articles every working day.

Vehicles

For every 1,000 people in Australia, there are over 500 motor vehicles. Most families have at least one car and it is the normal means of transport for work, business and leisure for millions of Australians.

While you can usually commute to work by public transport, as long as you work the standard rat-race hours, you may find yourself lost at weekends when your friends are whizzing off for a couple of days down the country. With the suburbanisation of shopping centres, you will miss out on the best value and choice if you have to shop in the city centre for lack of transport.

One good point about driving is that petrol costs about the same in Australian dollars as it does here in pounds, so it costs half as much. But with the distances involved, it would want to.

Lots of people buy a car immediately on arrival in Australia, hardly stopping to unpack first. Others spend a year there without buying one. The choice really depends on your own situation. Migrants arriving in the city where they intend to settle are going to need one sooner or later and may as well buy it sooner. If they do not have work lined up, it will help to be able to work anywhere within a reasonable distance – something not always possible using public transport.

On the other hand, working holidaymakers will find that they can pay for quite a few hire-cars and taxis with the price of buying and running a car. One extra point to consider, for those arriving in Perth and intending to travel around, is that it is a very, very long way to anywhere. If you buy a car there, it must be in pretty good condition if you want to bring it east.

Car Hire

Hiring a car can be a way of getting a weekend away from the city, or of breaking away from the main public transport routes when you are on holiday. With a group of you sharing it can work out pretty cheap. The three major national car-hire companies are Avis, Hertz and Budget. Then there are a host of smaller companies that operate only in one city, town or even from only one garage.

There is strong competition in the car-hire business, so look

out for special deals. Try a couple of places and ask each of
them for a deal or a cut. Anything more than two days should
qualify for some discount off the standard daily rate – ask
about weekend, weekly or four-day rentals.

The big companies offer newer cars, greater choice and
special features like one-way rentals (driving a car from one
city to another) and airport pick-ups. Their lowest rates range
upwards from $40 a day. The opposition, the smaller com-
panies, will usually have older cars, but you can normally get
a car from them for about $30 a day, basic.

There are lots of things to take into account when picking
a company and striking a bargain. You must usually choose
between a city rental (with unlimited kilometres) and a
country rental (where you pay from 18 cents a kilometre and
may or may not get the first couple of hundred free). Insurance may or may not be included in the quoted price, usually
it is not. As well as the standard insurance, you can pay extra
for insurance to cover your liability for the first several
hundred dollars of any claim, known as a collision damage
waiver. Check too whether there are any special restrictions
on where you can use the car. Some companies hire little
two-cylinder Handyvans, but will not let you take them outside
the town. In other areas, like far north Queensland, the
Northern Territory and northern WA, you will probably want
to use gravel roads. Most hire contracts have a woolly clause
about using the car on 'unmade' roads. Find out exactly what
they mean.

Car-hire companies prefer credit cards to cash, but most
will take cash too. When you have chosen a company, bring
in your licence(s) and sign a credit-card charge docket which
is put away until you return. Ask about the rules for petrol
(usually full tank out, full tank back) and away you go. You
may of course tear off up goat tracks, ford rivers and go bush
in your hired car, but going outside your area of use may void
your insurance and you will be in deep trouble if you break
down or crash while driving somewhere you were not sup-
posed to be in the first place.

Mokes

These are little, semi-open tin boxes on wheels that are often
cheaper to hire than cars. They are great fun in a warm place

and well worth hiring for a day, just for fun. Remember though, that they only look like four-wheel drives, they are not meant for off-road driving. They give you very little protection in a crash and there is really no place to lock your valuables in a Moke.

Motor cycles
Motor cycles are very popular in Australia, and one can understand why when the main drawback, the rain, is missing for much of the year. They are cheaper to buy than in Ireland, but all the other disadvantages are there – bike-blind drivers in cars and trucks, potential vandalism and a high rate of death and injury among bike riders. If you are considering touring, go for a good big four-stroke. The distances are just too great for smaller machines.

Buying a Car

Buying a car carries the same pitfalls in Australia as in Ireland, with a couple of extra ones. You have three ways to go; private sales, dealers and auctions. This is, of course, for second-hand cars. If you have the money for a new car, you will get lots of advice for free from the car salesmen.

Private sales and auctions will be cheaper for any given year and model, but it is that much harder to check the car out thoroughly if it is in an auction yard and you are allowed to do no more than look at it. Private sellers are not obliged to give you any sort of guarantee.

Used-car salesmen (they refer to the cars as 'pre-owned') are the same the world over – they would go to great lengths to turn a quid. Do not take their word for anything. On the other hand, dealers are covered by the local guarantee system and with a registered dealer you can be sure of the title of the car. That is, you can be sure he owns the car he is selling you. You can run into big problems if the car you buy in a private sale turns out to have thousands owing on it to a hire-purchase company. Unfortunately, there is no easy way to establish that the private individual selling a car actually owns it.

The guarantee system
The guarantee system varies from State to State and depends on the price of the car. In WA, for example, where the most

basic guarantee comes in at $1,500, you see an awful lot of cars on sale for $1,499. Check the terms of the guarantee system in the State where you intend to buy. The best source of advice on things vehicular is the State motoring organisation. Join as soon as you are sure you want to buy a car.

State motoring organisations
The motoring organisations are: the National Roads and Motorists' Association (NSW); the Automobile Association of the Northern Territory; the Royal Automobile Club of Queensland; the Royal Automobile Club of South Australia; the Royal Automobile Club of Western Australia; the Royal Automobile Club of Tasmania; the Royal Automobile Club of Victoria. For an annual fee of about $40, they will provide towing, insurance opportunities, advice and mechanical inspections. Your organisation will detail the guarantee scheme in your State and most publish a leaflet on buying a used car.

Unless you are mechanically expert, it is worth the $50 or so that the motoring organisations charge to thoroughly check out the car you are thinking of buying. If the seller will not allow you to have it inspected, be suspicious, particularly when you are talking about an expensive (over $4,000) car.

The organisations will also tell you the legal requirements for buying a car. In NSW, for example, each car sold must have a pink slip certifying its roadworthiness. If the owner has already got one, so much the better. In WA, on the other hand, the car need only be inspected if the registration has been allowed to lapse and you want to renew it, so buy a car that is still registered. Re-registering a car from another State can be a hassle, so buy one registered in the State you are in.

Prices vary, but you can get mobile for under $1,000. It is only recently that the bargain-hunter's ideal of the $500 car that just goes and goes faded away. Anything under $1,000 is going to be an ancient heap. Many such cars date from the early 1970s and have the big, thirsty six-cylinder engines that were standard in Australia at the time. Even with the low price of petrol, they can be costly on long trips. On the other hand, you may be lucky.

For $2,000, you should get a more recent model, perhaps only ten years old, with some sort of guarantee. Three thousand should buy you a reasonable car. If the dealer tries to pooh pooh the statutory warranty and give you a forte warranty, tell him to shove it up his singlet. The forte warranty makes very expensive demands on the owner about servicing and maintenance in order to have any validity at all.

Stamp duty is payable on the sale of second-hand cars and is related to their price. Therefore, many buyers and sellers prepare a second receipt which understates the price (within reason). The practice is illegal, but widespread.

Time was when you were crazy to buy anything but a Holden car if you intended going outside the cities in Australia. It was far easier to get spares for them. This is becoming less and less true. Chances are now that you will be able to get parts for established Japanese models like the Toyota Corolla quite easily. However, the Holden parts may be available on an abandoned car or from a breaking yard at a lower price than the new Japanese spare.

Registration and Insurance
In Australia, the legally required basic third-party personal injury insurance is included with the registration. Registration is like our road tax here, except that more Australians have it and the police do a better job of keeping unregistered drivers off the road. Registration costs vary from State to State, but it is worth buying a car with some months left to run on its registration.

Even though registration covers your legal need for insurance, it is worth paying at least for third-party damage cover. You can run up quite a bill by writing off someone else's brand new car in a collision. Insurance costs are nothing like the ridiculous ones we face in Ireland.

Outback Driving

There are problems to look out for if you are going to drive in the outback. It is only in the 1980s that sealed roads were completed right around Australia and from Darwin down to Adelaide. Many of the smaller roads are extremely rough. For long trips in remote areas, stick to the sealed highway.

Take elementary precautions before heading off. Pack basic spares, (fan-belt, spare oil, etc.) and the tools to fit them. Make sure your car is sound, not forgetting the tyres and the spare. If you are not using one of the main highways, ensure that the one you want to use is suitable for your vehicle and that there is plenty of petrol available along it. Carry plenty of water. You can collapse from dehydration very quickly in the inland desert in summer. Many people also carry a second spare tyre and a temporary windscreen, if travelling in remote areas.

On the road

Distances in Australia are enormous, so plan for stop-overs. Beware of fatigue too. One stretch of the Perth-Adelaide highway runs over ninety miles without a bend of any sort. It can be mesmerising and sleep-making, but gum trees are very unyielding things to hit at speed.

Almost as unyielding are the animals. A kangaroo can weigh enough to write off your car if you hit one. You will notice a lot of Australian cars have 'roo-bars' on the front to fend them off, but even these do not offer complete protection as the animal can come through the windscreen or the impact with the bar can twist the chassis of the car. The answer adopted by most Australians is to drive only in daylight hours in roo-full areas. Watch out too for cattle, buffaloes, wild horses and donkeys, camels and wombats.

On a long trip, look out for the signs telling you where your next petrol is. It is no fun at all to hitch a hundred miles to fetch petrol after you run out. Last, but not least, among the dangers are road trains. These are articulated lorries of up to four trailers and up to 50 metres in length. Give them plenty of space and do not under-estimate the amount of space you need to pass one. Look out too for the yards where the road trains are put together (they are not allowed into cities without being broken up).

9 Dunnies, Dingoes and Dinky Dis. . . The language.

One explanation for the Australian accent says that it comes of having to keep the lips close together to keep the flies out. Whatever about that theory, there are certainly enough colourful words and expressions to make you wonder sometimes whether English and Australian are one and the same language. Here is a short introduction to the wonderful world of strine – Australia's own language. Words of Aboriginal origin are marked (A).

Abo	Aboriginal, offensive, but commonly used.
Amber fluid	beer.
Arvo	afternoon.
Award	salary, rate of pay.
Back of Bourke	far away, remote.
Bail up	hold up, rob.
Banana bender	Queenslander.
Barbie	barbecue.
Barramundi (A)	the giant perch, *Lates calcarifer*, great sport and very good to eat.
Bathers	swimming togs.
Battler	a fighter, someone who has to struggle to get by.
Beaut!	that's good!
Bewdie	like beaut.
Bikie	motorcyclist.
Blowie or blowfly	bluebottle.
Bludger	scrounger, as in dole-bludger.
Blue	a row.
Bond	deposit.
Boomerang (A)	curved throwing weapon, you know, as recorded by early settlers.
Bonzer	good.
Boong	Aboriginal, offensive, but common.
Bottle shop	off-licence.
Brumby (A)	wild horse.
Bush	country, as in 'go bush' and 'bushed' (lost)

BYO	Bring Your Own, a restaurant to which you bring your own wine or beer.
Chiko Roll	revolting type of fast food.
Chook	chicken.
Chunder	vomit.
Cockie	small farmer, also cockatoo.
Cooee	what you call when you're bushed.
Compo	compensation.
Cozzy	swimming gear, from costume.
Crim	criminal.
Crook	unwell, equally for people, animals and cars.
Currawong (A)	a large black bird, *Strepera graculina.*
Cut-Lunch	sandwiches.
Dag, daggy	dirt that clings to a sheep's rear, also a term of abuse.
Damper	flour and water mix, cooked on a stick in a fire in the bush.
Dill	fool.
Dilly, Dillybag (A)	formerly a native woven bag, extended to mean European-style bags.
Dingo (A)	a wild dog, a term of abuse for people.
Dinky di	a 'real' Australian.
Dob in	to inform on.
Double dip	to cheat, as in claiming dole and working.
Drongo	useless person.
Duna	duvet.
Dunny	toilet.
Durex	one to watch. . . adhesive tape.
Fair dinkum	true, straight up.
Fair go	an appeal to someone's sense of fair play.
Financial	in the money.
Flake	shark meat.
Floater	fast food, consisting of a meat pie floating in pea soup, topped with tomato ketchup.
Fossick	prospect for gold or gems, to potter around.
Galah	silly person, from pink bird.
Garbo	a bin-man, and similarly, postie, milko.
G'day	hello – yes, they really say it.
Give it away	give it up, quit.
God botherer	religious person, especially missionary or charismatic.

Good on yer	well done.
Grazier	big farmer.
Grog	drink.
Hoon	rogue, lair.
Humpy	Aboriginal shelter.
Interstate	every state except the one you are in.
Jackaroo	cowboy, female equivalent is a jillaroo.
Joey	young kangaroo.
Journo	you guessed it, a journalist.
Koala (A)	tree-dwelling marsupial with a far better public image than it deserves.
Kookaburra (A)	large kingfisher, *Dacelo gigas*, famous for its lovely call that sounds like a laugh.
Lamington	small, square cake, invented in Australia.
Lair	layabout, ruffian.
Larrikin	a rogue.
Layby	to put a deposit on something in a shop.
Lollies	sweets, and lolly-water, lemonade.
Lurk	a plan or racket, often entertained by a 'lurk merchant'.
Mallee (A)	eucalypt shrub, also a district.
Manchester	linen and sheet department in a store.
Mate	friend, on the one hand one of the most valued institutions of Australian male life, mateship. Other people just use it like a full stop, to end every sentence.
Mick	a Catholic.
Mozzie	mosquito.
Never never	real outback, back of Bourke.
New Australian	recent immigrant.
No worries	that's OK, that's right.
Ocker	crude Australian stereotype, offensive.
Off-sider	helper, assistant.
OS	overseas, as in he met her OS.
Pademelon (A)	small wallaby (which, in turn, is a small macropod or kangaroo-like animal).
Pastoralist	large farmer.
Polly	politician.
Pom	British person, often in the phrase 'whingeing Pom'.
Push	group of larrikins, a gang.

Rage	social event.
Ramp, Rort	scheme, racket, sharp practice.
Ratbag	untrustworthy.
Ratshit	not very good.
Retrench	to make redundant, to lay off.
Ripper	great, fantastic.
Road train	three-section juggernaut.
Root	to copulate. If you say harmless things like 'rooting in a drawer' dinki di Aussies will fall around laughing.
Schooner	large beer glass, there are also ponies, pots, butchers and middies.
Sea Wasp	the deadly box-jellyfish.
Sealed road	surfaced road.
See you later	means goodbye, with no necessary intention of ever seeing someone again.
Shit-hot	good.
Shithouse	bad.
Shoot through	leave in a hurry.
Sickie	sick leave from work.
Smoko	short break from work.
Squatter	large land-owning farmer.
Stickybeak	nosey person, have a stickybeak means to have a snoop.
Stubby	small bottle of beer.
Stuffed	of a person, in bad way, tired. Of an object, broken.
Sunbake	sunbathe.
Surfies	surfing fanatics.
Taipan (A)	the very venomous snake, *Oxyranus scutellatus*.
Tall poppies	achievers, targets for begrudgers.
Technicolour yawn	vomit.
Tinny	can of beer.
Thongs	what we call flip-flops. Universal Aussie summer wear.
Tucker	food.
Two-up	mad Australian gambling game, as seen in *Crocodile Dundee*.
True blue	genuine Australian.

Up himself	superior, snobbish.
Ute	Utility, or open-backed truck.
Walkabout	to give away responsibilities and wander off, to disappear.
Wet, the	monsoon season up north.
Wharfie	docker.
Whinge	to moan, to complain.
Wog	anyone to whom English is a second language.
Wowser	a spoilsport, a prude.
Yabby (A)	freshwater, prawn-like fish, delicious.
Yakka (A)	work, as in 'hard yakka'.
Youi (A)	yes.
Your shout	your round.

10 What's Where – Cities and States

Sydney

The establishment of a penal colony at Sydney Cove in 1788 is seen as the beginning of modern Australia. This is the event to be celebrated in 1988 with the country's bicentennial. Sydney is Australia's largest and oldest city, with a population of almost 3.5 million and a sprawling metropolis with a busy modern heart. Perhaps its most striking feature is the amount of high-rise buildings in the central business district. With the lifting of height restrictions in 1957 Sydney just shot upwards. Highest of these is Centre Point Tower. Open to the public – for a fee – the view from the top gives a very good orientation to the city. You can see the harbour, beaches and endless undulating suburbs, with the Blue Mountains in the distance, the features for which Sydney is loved. Sydney's most well-known landmarks are the Opera House and the Harbour Bridge. Built in 1932, the Harbour Bridge provides the main traffic artery from the northern suburbs to the city centre, it is crossed by an enormous number of cars each day. A pylon can be climbed if you are prepared to brave the traffic fumes and pay 50 cents. You can walk across it for nothing. The view of the harbour – though slightly obscured by an anti-suicide fence – is worth the effort.

Ferries are another of Sydney's major attractions. They leave from Circular Quay and a trip to the suburb of Manley or Taronga Park Zoo – if you cannot afford to actually live on the harbour and commute by ferry every day – should not be missed.

Sydney has a number of old buildings which have been beautifully restored. The Rocks area is interesting to wander around and contains an Irish pub, 'The Molly Malone' bar in the Mercantile Hotel.

The main shopping street is George Street, the most interesting feature of which is the Queen Victoria Building, a lavishly restored market building which now houses expensive shops and restaurants. The statue of Queen Victoria which once graced the lawns of Leinster House is to be installed in the QVB shortly. Nearby is the Town Hall, which has a huge organ, with pipes covering one whole wall.

As well as Hyde Park, a rather over-used square in the city centre, notable only for the wild possums which inhabit its trees and frighten unsuspecting lovers on park benches, Sydney has the Domain and Botanical Gardens, a huge area beside the Opera House which is a very pleasant escape from the busy, noisy, rather dirty city centre.

Kings Cross is the sleazy area, full of sex shops and cheap accommodation. A handy place to live if you are in Sydney for a short while, it contains much of the city's nightlife. Oxford Street, leading to Paddington and the eastern suburbs, is another rather rundown street of restaurants, shops and pubs (many gay).

Bondi has to be Sydney's most famous suburb. The beach is small and rather scruffy, but here you may see the surfers and beach culture – golden, tanned people, keep-fit fanatics, surf life-saving clubs going through daring manoeuvres, watched by busloads of Japanese tourists.

There is a lot to see and do in Sydney and most tourists will visit it at some stage, if only because they feel it has to be done. As a city to live in, it has tremendous potential for career and social opportunities, with of course the attendant problems (mostly of street crime, pollution and godforsaken suburbs) apparent in any large urban mass. For those who crave the bright lights and excitement in Australia, Sydney is the place to be.

New South Wales

New South Wales is the most populous, most industrialised and most highly urbanised of the States. With a population of about 5.5 million it covers an area of $801,600 \, km^2$ or 10.4% of the total area of Australia. It provides 36% of all goods manufactured in the country and 24% of Australia's mining products. As well as Sydney there are two other large industrial centres, Newcastle and Wollongong. Eighty kilometres south of Sydney, Wollongong has a population of over 236,000 and became notorious during 1987 for an outbreak of Legionnaires Disease.

The countryside in New South Wales ranges from rich agricultural land, through plains and sheep country, to dusty outback. The coastal region provides sheltered resorts and dramatic scenery, Byron Bay and Coffs Harbour are two especially popular spots. As with much in Australia, the State's size means variety is the name of the game. The Hunter Valley is the centre of the wine industry. Griffith, a major agricultural and market gardening centre, has a large Italian population and was at one time the hub of a thriving marijuana industry. In the north-west of New South Wales, towards the Queensland border, is an area of dry plains and dust, the centre of which, Bourke, (800 km NW of Sydney) is a byword for the real outback.

Broken Hill, a mining town 1170 km west of Sydney, provides an oasis of interest in a bleak landscape. This, the far west of New South Wales is also dry dusty country, but it contains remnants of earlier mining days and Aboriginal settlements.

The area south-west of Sydney, moving towards Melbourne, is mostly pastoral and agricultural. Goulburn and Albury are the major population centres of this quiet farming country. The Murray River forms much of the boundary between NSW and Victoria.

The Murray River and its tributaries, the Darling, Murrumbidgee, Lachlan, Goulburn and many small rivers, has a catchment area which extends not only over much of New South Wales but also over a large part of southern Queensland and much of Victoria. It is the largest river system in Australia. About 80% of the country's irrigated land is within this river system and 60% of the exploitable surface water is used. All around the system are areas of fruit, vegetable and grape production.

Melbourne

Melbourne was founded in 1835 and ever since has been vying with Sydney. Of similar size, with a population of over 2.9 million, it is always considered to be Australia's second most important city. For years it was the main centre for banking and finance in Australia, though its importance in this area is diminishing. Very different to Sydney, it is a city of substantial, grey buildings and wide, straight streets. Often compared to a city in Europe, especially Paris, its weather is the subject of many jokes. It does rain a lot in Melbourne, though many say it is a friendlier, more lively city in which to live than any of the others. There is a substantial Greek population and many Asians, especially Vietnamese, have settled there.

Of particular interest is its National Gallery. This is acknowledged to have the greatest collection of Australian romantic paintings. Historic buildings include the Royal Mint and St James Cathedral (1872 and 1842 respectively) beside Flagstaff Gardens, and the Old Melbourne Gaol, now a penal museum. It contains death masks of famous bushrangers and convicts, and Ned Kelly's armour. The Victoria Market is excellent for cheap fruit and vegetables, on Sundays it becomes a general market. It is on the corner of Peel and Victoria Streets in North Melbourne.

The tram system in Melbourne is the main source of public transport. Attractive, old-fashioned and jolting, a ride in one is not to be missed — most typically at rush hour when they are crammed impossibly full of sweating humanity. They are symbols of Melbourne in the way the Opera House is of Sydney. The most interesting suburbs of Melbourne are Carlton, inner-city and new-fashionable, Toorak, the most exclusive area, headquarters of the 'old money' for which Melbourne is famous — Toorak is to Melbourne what Montenotte is to Cork. St Kilda, the seaside suburb, is the sin centre. The city is the centre of Australia's motor vehicle industry and an important manufacturing centre. The port of Melbourne is the country's busiest general cargo port, though not the largest — Sydney has that distinction!

Victoria

Victoria is known as the 'Garden State'. With its area of rich soil and grasslands, particularly around the Murray River System, it produces 20% of Australia's total agricultural and pastoral output. Robinvale and Mildura (550 km from Melbourne), north towards the New South Wales border, are major centres for the growth of grapes and citrus fruit. Further to the north-west is the Mallee region, an area of unproductive, dry bushland and sparse population which gets even emptier and bleaker as you move towards Broken Hill in NSW. The rest of the countryside around the Murray River would be similar to this, were it not for the major irrigation schemes started in the latter part of the nineteenth century.

To the west of Melbourne is the rich sheep and pastoral country of the Western District, stretching as far as the South Australian border. Hamilton is the centre of this area which was the cause of explorer Thomas Mitchell describing the country as 'Australia Felix' – the lucky country.

The Mornington Peninsula and Phillip Island, south-east of Melbourne, are popular resort areas with good beaches. Further along the south coast is Wilson's Promontory, containing a good National Park. The western coastline is more spectacular and rugged, with pretty coastal towns which were once centres of the whaling industry.

Another industrial city in Victoria is Geelong – population 130,000, south-west of Melbourne. Victoria is not all attractive countryside, it is an important manufacturing State, holding one-third of Australia's total means of industrial production, based mostly in Melbourne, Geelong, and the Latrobe Valley.

Adelaide

The population of Adelaide is under one million. Estimated in 1984 to be 978,900, this comparatively small number is reflected in the quietness of the city's streets and the relaxed, almost provincial atmosphere of the city centre. Adelaide is a beautiful sunny city, on the banks of the Torrens River, flanked by the hills of the Mount Lofty ranges. It used to be known as 'the city of churches' and it does have many attractive old churches. It also has a modern Festival Centre, located on the south bank of the Torrens, where Australia's premier Arts Festival is held every second year. 1988 is one of those years and it will take place over three weeks in late February – early March, with guest performers and speakers from all over the world participating in dance, drama, music, art and workshop events. Adelaide is a well-planned city, with wide streets of imposing stone buildings. The effect is similar to Melbourne, but somehow lighter and cleaner, perhaps because the stone used is paler in colour.

North Adelaide is one of the most fashionable suburbs full

of restored bluestone houses, Melbourne Street is its exclusive shopping street. The seaside suburb of Glenelg is somewhat similar to, but less run-down than, Bray, Co Wicklow; it can be reached on Adelaide's only tram-line, which departs from Victoria Square. Not to be missed is the long winding drive up to the peak of Mount Lofty. This takes you through the hill suburbs, devastated in the 1983 bushfires. You need a car – or bicycle if you are super-fit – but the view from the mountain-top platform of the whole city, suburbs and sea stretched out below you is worth the effort.

Adelaide is a very pleasant city in which to live, with its attractive layout and buildings, a green belt of park-land around the city, and nearby hills and wineries to which you could escape from the rigours of work. Perhaps rather peaceful for some tastes, the presence of two universities (Flinders and Adelaide) should provide more than enough young people to ensure a lively social scene.

Australian Formula One Grand Prix

The first Grand Prix took place here in 1985 and was such a success it has been repeated annually in late October or early November. For five days the town is taken over by the world of motor racing and food and accommodation become scarce and expensive. The race is actually run through the city's streets and is a must for anyone interested in this sport.

South Australia

South Australia was established as a colony by a private company in 1836. It differs from the other States in that it was never a penal settlement, with the free convict labour for public building that that system entailed. Instead, the nurture of private enterprise and personal industriousness has left its mark on the many small-scale farms and wineries, carefully planted trees and well-kept, tamed countryside evident in many parts of South Australia.

From the early days, this State came under German influence, beginning with Lutherans settling there in 1839 to escape religious persecution in Europe. Hahndorf, a town 29 km south-east of Adelaide, is very Germanic, and worth a visit although it is very touristy.

The resident population of South Australia is around

1,358,000. Most live in Adelaide or the other industrial centres. Elizabeth is a satellite town of Adelaide, a centre of the motor manufacturing industry. Whyalla, on the west coast of the Eyre Peninsula is an important steel-producing centre and deep-water port. Port Augusta, at the head of the Spencer Gulf, is a crossroads for goods and people going in all directions and an electricity generating centre.

The more densely populated agricultural areas are around the Murray River System, the centre of which is Renmark, 295 km from Adelaide. South Australia is best known for its wine production. If you enjoy visiting wineries the Barossa Valley (50 km south-east of Adelaide) will be of interest. The major town in the south-east is Mount Gambier (population 20,000).

South Australia has always been a very agricultural State, though this is changing, with primary production now employing only 7% of the workforce. Of the gross value of Australia's agricultural production this State contributes 13% in crops, 11% in livestock products and 9% in livestock slaughterings. Major agricultural products are wheat, barley, wine, beef, lamb and wool. Interestingly, it is also the driest State. Its arid climate means only 10% of the land is usable for cropping or permanent pasture.

As you move further north, you get into extremely desolate country of searing heat and dry salt lakes. The route towards Alice Springs from Adelaide is worth travelling, especially if you can pass through Coober Pedy, an opal-mining town which is mostly built underground to escape the heat.

To the far west of the State is fairly flat grain country, eventually becoming the expanse of the Nullarbor Desert, the huge land barrier between South Australia and Western Australia.

Hobart

Hobart is the second-oldest, the smallest and the furthest south State capital. Originally founded at Risdon Cove in 1803, the colony was moved about 10 km down the river the following year. There it, or at least its centre, remains, on the Derwent River, under the shadow of 1,270-metre Mount Wellington.

Today it is a bustling city of 180,000 people. Those who feel a longing for Irish weather should consider a visit. It rains on an average of 162 days a year, more than any other State capital, and it rarely gets hot in summer. In winter, it gets quite cold.

Much of the old town centre, far more than in most Australian cities, remains intact. The presence of convict (for which read 'free' or even 'slave') labour in its early days meant that substantial public, commercial and private buildings were possible. The activity of the town centred on the port in its early days as fortunes were made in whaling, ship-building and in exporting the rich produce of Tasmania. From this time, the buildings of Salamanca Place and Battery Point, down by the harbour, remain.

It is also worth visiting the Cadbury's factory, which must have one of the most beautiful factory sites in the world, on a bend in the Derwent. Regrettably they charge an admission fee ($5 in early 1987). Other points of interest are the Tasmanian Museum and Art Gallery, in Hobart's oldest building, the Commissariat Store built in 1808, and the 1811 Anglesea Barracks. The barracks is still used by the army, but is open to the public, free of charge, on weekdays.

Tasmania

Over 40% of Tasmanians live in and around Hobart, which leaves the rest of the island's 68,000 km^2 relatively lightly populated. Indeed, much of the west coast, particularly the south-western end is wilderness, with no settlements of any size.

Tasmania's major products are woodchip, paper and wood products, foodstuffs and chocolate from the huge Cadbury factory in Hobart. Fishing and tourism are also important income earners. Because of its natural abundance of suitable sites for hydro-electric generation, Tasmania also sells electricity. One of the most striking things for the Irish visitor is how like Ireland it is.

Probably Tasmania's biggest attraction for tourists is its wilderness. The most famous bushwalk in Australia, the Cradle Mountain – Lake St Clair overland track is mentioned in 'Seven things not to miss' but there are many other areas to be explored on foot. Maria Island, off the east coast is a peaceful wildlife sanctuary in which you can see wallabies, kangaroos and Cape Barron geese at close range.

The central west coast bears the scars of the attitude that has been all too common in the white man's dealings with Australia – dig it up, chop it down and flog it. There are a whole range of mines and mining towns, some still producing, others deserted. The hills around the town of Queenstown have been turned into a moonscape of bare rock by mining.

Also on the west coast is the port of Strahan, the base for cruises up the beautiful Gordon River. When the river is high enough, the cruises go right up to the junction with the Franklin River, where the State government intended flooding thousands of acres of virgin forest to generate yet more electricity. The plan was abandoned after pressure from the Federal govenment and a world-wide outcry.

In the south-eastern corner of Tasmania is the Tasman Peninsula, with the remains of the convict settlement at Port Arthur. It was with great glee the British discovered that the peninsula was a natural prison and in 1830 it was chosen as a place to confine prisoners who had committed crimes in the colony. The neck of the peninsula is narrow enough for the authorities to have chained dogs at intervals across it to make escape impossible.

Among the best-preserved buildings is the cottage in which William Smith O'Brien lived during his time there and the horrible Pentonville-style radial prison, designed to break the spirits of 'difficult' prisoners, or drive them mad by sensory deprivation.

Tasmania is well set up with campsites and hostels. There are a great many things to see and none of them is too far from the rest. These facts, and the friendliness of many local people, make up for the extra trouble and expense of getting there from the mainland.

Brisbane

Brisbane is situated in the south-eastern corner of Queensland about 30 km inland from Moreton Bay. Of similar size to Perth, with a population of about one million, it is a more bustling city. This is possibly because of its role as a gateway to the heavily promoted tourists' paradise that is Queensland. Brisbane is the jumping-off point for the coastal resorts of the Gold Coast, Sunshine Coast and the Great Barrier Reef.

The city was established as a penal colony in 1824 and remained one until 1842. During that time no free men were allowed within 80 km of the city. It was eventually thrown open for free settlement after pressure from jealous would-be settlers who could see its potential – this spirit of entrepreneurship is still apparent in the business world of Brisbane today.

The city has an interesting mixture of old and new buildings and is given character by the gentle hills sloping up from the big loop in the Brisbane River upon which it is based. The City Hall (1930) is a huge building which houses the city's entire civic organisation. On Anne Street, the square immediately in front of it, (King George Square) is in many ways the focal point of the central city area. Most important of Brisbane's public buildings is the Cultural Centre. Located in South Brisbane, on the banks of the river, it is a major new development containing the Museum, Art Gallery, auditoria and restaurants and a huge exhibition centre. It is to be completed in time for an international exposition, Expo 88.

Expo 88 is due to be held from March to October 1988. On the theme 'leisure in the age of technology' it is to be one of Queensland's attractions in the bicentennial year. More than six million people are expected to visit the exposition and there will be major international participation. It is hoped that at least 30 countries will be involved.

There are short cruises and day-trips available on the river. Koala-fanciers would enjoy a trip to the Lone Pine Koala Sanctuary, one of the many places where you can cuddle the creatures. Even John-Paul II held a koala on his visit to Australia in 1986.

Brisbane is not a major manufacturing centre, though it does have a busy port with trade in containers, bulk cement and sugar. It is a major convention centre, though, with many big hotels and conference facilities. Its capacity in this area was boosted in 1982, when it hosted the Commonwealth Games.

With a wide choice of restaurants and some very fashionable shops, Brisbane would be a good choice of city in which to live. It has plenty of sunshine – an average seven-and-a-half hours of it a day, an interesting ethnic mix, a good location for holidays and weekends away, and is small enough to be friendly yet large enough to be a lively place. One drawback is that work – unless perhaps in the tourist trade – and reasonably priced long-term accommodation seem to be hard to come by.

Queensland

Queensland is second only to Western Australia in size. It covers 22.5% of the continent and has a total area of 1,728,000 km^2. Totally unlike Western Australia, it has a sizeable population and a number of thriving regional centres and industrial towns as well as Brisbane. It is the third most populous state, with a population of over 2,525,000 – 16% of the total population of Australia.

Agriculture, mining, manufacturing and tourism are all important industries. Queensland is a major source of income for Australia, producing 23% of the total value of Australia's exports. If you also remember that Queensland is a favourite holiday destination for both native Australians and overseas tourists you may realise that it is a good source of casual work. Some seasonal jobs, in agriculture or tourism, will be available somewhere in Queensland all year round. The difficulty, with such a huge State, may be in picking the right place at the right time.

Queensland's Image

The State is cleverly marketed by a series of economic and tourism development agencies aided by an active State Government. As with New South Wales, Queensland is a State of infinite variety, with somewhere to suit all needs and tastes. It is also more exotic than the staider, colder more southerly States. This is aided by its climate – more than half of the State lies within the tropics and this results in an excitingly different flora and fauna and agricultural produce. It is also seen as separate, somehow apart from the rest of Australia. People make Queensland jokes as we make Kerry jokes, they call Queenslanders 'banana benders' but underlying this condescension is an almost envious regard for the State's differences.

Geographical Outline

Geographically, the State of Queensland can be divided into four main sections. From the Gold Coast resort area on the New South Wales border to the outpost of Cooktown on the Cape York Peninsula in far North Queensland is the coastal strip, with almost endless beaches, many small islands and, from Townsville onwards, the Great Barrier Reef. Surfer's Paradise, the centre of the Gold Coast and Noosa, the centre of the Sunshine Coast, are Australia's answer to Benidorm or Torremolinos, all high-rise holiday apartments and amusement arcades. Perfect resorts if you enjoy that kind of place, they have one drawback. The high-rise apartments are so tall they sometimes cut the sun off the beaches in the early afternoon.

The further north you go along this coast the more deserted and tropical the beaches become. Crocodiles also become more frequent further north. Daintree (90 km north of Cairns, as far as you can go up this coast on a surfaced road) has a thriving tourist trade based on cruises to spot these unappealing reptiles.

There are a number of sizeable towns on the coastal strip, most of which are dependent on the tourist trade and used principally as departure points for islands and popular holiday spots along the coast. Important agricultural centres and also of interest to the tourist are: Maryborough (population 20,200, timber and sugar industries), Bundaberg (population 32,700, sugar, tobacco, fruit industries – and of course the knock-out, over-proof rum), Rockhampton (population 51,200, beef centre), Mackay (population 35,600, sugar processing and export, coal export). Sugar is one of Queensland's major agricultural products. It produces 95% of Australia's total production. Everywhere one is surrounded by waving fields of sugar cane.

Inland from the coastal strip, the gentle slopes of the Great Dividing Range eventually give way to the rich agricultural tablelands region. Here, more sugar is grown, also peanuts, all kinds of tropical fruit, vegetables and grain. The Darling Downs is Australia's most fertile area of grain production, the centre of which is Toowoomba (population 64,000). As one moves further west and north, the vast plains of productive soil gradually give way to harsh countryside, flat and sparsely populated. This area is difficult to travel, with mostly unsurfaced roads and numerous dry riverbeds which flood periodically.

Mount Isa is the only major settlement in the outback, and it exists only because it is the site of one of the world's richest mines and the only one in the world where copper, silver, lead and zinc are found in quantity together. It is 887 km west of Townsville with a population of 24,000.

Perth

Perth is spacious and clean, with lots of parks. The wide stretches of the Swan River and other waterways around which it is built make it appear more like a purpose-built holiday resort than a city. The city centre itself is quite small, with a lot of soulless glass and concrete high-rise buildings. Very few of the city's old, quaint or historically significant buildings have survived the economic expansion of the last 25 years.

Sunny, with an excellent climate, Perth's major attractions are its parks and gardens, unpolluted beaches and the Swan River, all of which make for an outdoor, water-sport orientated existence. There are several wineries on the Swan River, about 25 km from Perth, and a cruise (from Barrack Street jetty, in the city centre) to one of these is an interesting, if rather debauched experience. Among the beaches are Cottesloe, City Beach and Scarborough, each of which is nicer and cleaner than the world-famous Bondi in Sydney. The Swan River provides a venue for para-gliding, windsurfing and sailing, all very close to the city centre. Kings Park is a large tract of natural bushland and green parkland, also containing the Botanical Gardens within walking distance of the city centre. Stirling Gardens, on the corner of Barrack Street and St Georges Terrace is a pleasant small park, as beloved of office workers as St Stephen's Green.

Perth's most interesting suburb is Fremantle, the original port for the city. It has the character and interesting old buildings, including many pubs, that the city centre lacks. Restored for the America's Cup in 1986, it is very much a young people's centre. There is a market there on Saturdays and Sundays.

Perth's most exclusive suburb is Dalkeith where the riverside mansions are the homes of the many millionaires of which Perth has a higher concentration than any other Australian city. The city is backed by the Darling Range of hills and is fringed by market gardens and soft-fruit farms. Rottnest Island, just off the coast, is a popular weekend destination. It is the only home of the Quokka, a unique marsupial that looks like a cross between a rat and a squirrel.

Perth would be a clean, relaxed city in which to live, with tremendous potential for those who like outdoor sports. Its isolation and size do make it quiet and limited in terms of work opportunity and night life – especially in comparison to the major cities of the Eastern States.

Perth's Isolation

It is only in recent years that Perth has experienced major growth, largely as a result of exploiting Western Australia's mineral wealth. It is still only the marketing and staging post for the rich fields of iron-ore, nickel, oil and natural gas, many minerals and gold which are located in remote regions and off the coast in the far north and west of the State. Perth is still not a major manufacturing centre – in all of Western Australia there were only 4,000 establishments (employing 70,000 workers), in 1984, 80% of which were in the Perth area. Though this number has grown since then, mining-related work is still the city's biggest income earner.

The problem for Perth is the same now as when it was founded in 1829, and has to be considered in any discussion of the city. It is a very long way from anywhere else in Australia, with great areas of barren land and inhospitable desert forming a major transport and communications barrier, and it is the only major population centre in the State.

Western Australia

Western Australia is a massive state, with an area of 2,525,500 km^2, almost one-third the total area of Australia. It is also very sparsely populated, with about 1,500,000 people, the majority of whom live in the south-west corner in Perth and a few other small population centres, making up only 8.8% of Australia's population. It is also a rich state, earning 23% of the national export income. Its mineral production is one-third of the total Australian output.

Much of the countryside is very barren, with two major desert areas, the Nullarbor Plain extending to the South Australian border in the south-west and the Great Sandy Desert lying between the mountainous gorge country of the Pilbara and Kimberley regions in the north. Between these two are also the Gibson desert, extending to the Northern Territory border to the east and the Great Victoria Desert which runs as far as Coober Pedy in South Australia's far north.

The only real routes in Western Australia are right around the coast (there is a total 12,500 km of it), or the Eyre Highway which crosses the Nullarbor Plain to Adelaide, 2,824 km away. Most of the agricultural land is in the south-west corner. Wheat and sheep are the major products and Northam (population 6,800) and Narrogin (population 5,000) are major towns of the wheatlands. Near Hyden, an unusual rock formation called Wave Rock is a popular tourist destination. See it if in the area – it doesn't really warrant the lengthy trip from Perth in its own right.

Below Perth, towards the south-west extremity of the state, is rolling golden pastoral country, the fruit-producing areas of Donnybrook and the wineries of Margaret River, followed by the coastal towns of Albany and Esperance. At least one shark attack occurred in the Esperance area in 1987, but these towns remain popular holiday spots for the people of Perth. Absolutely unforgettable in this area are the towering Jarrah and Karri forests, eucalypt varieties which are among the hardest and most durable of the world's woods. The centre for visiting these is the town of Pemberton. They are beautiful tall straight trees which grow up to 60 metres high. Some of the tallest were used until quite recently as lookout posts for bushfires and you can climb one if you are feeling courageous.

North of Perth there is a lot of dry, flat bushland and some spectacular coastal scenery. Near Cervantes is the Pinnacles Desert. Further up the coast is Shark Bay, with the town of Denham (population 400) having the position of most westerly town in Australia. Twenty-six kilometres from Denham is Monkey Mia, where it is possible to play with schools of wild dolphins. Major places of interest further up this coast are few and very far between. The Pilbara region, with some impressive mountains and gorges, is an area of wild scenery. Broome is a pearling town with a developing tourist industry. Most of the other settlements in the far north are support towns for mining companies. The Kimberleys, the centre for which is Derby, is also an area of wild magnificence. Because distances are so vast in the north of Western Australia many people choose to fly between places of interest. About 600 km east of Perth, travelling towards Adelaide are the old gold mining towns, Coolgardie and Kalgoorlie (population 20,000). Kalgoorlie is still a booming gold town.

Western Australia's Wildflowers
In season (August to October) people travel from all over Australia to see the wildflowers of this State. Spectacular largely because of their quantity – they grow in profusion over vast areas – some are unique to the region. The most interesting, the Kangaroo Paw, is the symbol of Westen Australia and popularly cultivated as a garden plant.

Darwin

Darwin, on top of Australia's 'Top End', capital of the Northern Territory, is a strange city, perhaps both because of its relative youth as a place of any importance, which really only stems from its position as first line of defence in the Second World War, and the kind of people who choose to live there.

Darwin's population numbers about 67,000 and they must all be the kind of people who enjoy climatic extremes and geographical isolation. City-wise, Darwin has the most of everything: most sunshine (an average of 8.5 hours a day) most rainfall (annual average 1.536 millimetres), highest mean temperatures for both the hottest and coldest months (hottest month 29.6°C, coldest month 25.1°C – hardly cool!). It is also well-known for having the highest per-capita beer consumption in Australia.

Darwin is not only newly important, but also newly built. The resilience of the people who live there may be judged by the way they have twice rebuilt the city. It was almost completely destroyed by Japanese bombing raids during the Second World War and again by Cyclone Tracy in the early hours of Christmas morning 1974. The buildings of the new city are of undistinguished architecture and strangely scruffy

– Darwin doesn't seem to have the careful planning of Canberra or the glossy office buildings of Perth or Brisbane. It does have a character of its own and would be a fascinating city to visit or live in. It has a very transient work-force and is made more attractive by the tropical loading many pay awards contain. Casual work, especially fishing, labouring or in the tourist industry, appears to be relatively easy to come by.

Darwin's layout is made rather confusing by the site of its airport. Very close to the city centre, the suburbs have had to extend around it and most accommodation is a long way from the central city area. It is a good place in which to have a car, though public transport of a sort does exist.

The Northern Territory

The Northern Territory is a vast area of 1,346,200 km^2, 17.5% of the Australian continent. Most of this is empty outback, with remote cattle stations, few settlements or surfaced roads. The main roads stretch away through red dusty countryside, and the wide-open spaces and harsh environment through which they pass is in many ways the classical concept of the real Australia.

Eighty per cent of the Northern Territory's area is in the tropics. The area around Darwin has two seasons, wet and dry. Everywhere is hot during the day, but the central desert area, around Alice Springs, gets very cold at night – often below freezing point in winter. The Northern Territory's chief industries are mining (mostly of uranium and bauxite), tourism, beef cattle production and agriculture. Agricultural production is quite limited, it consists mostly of cash crops grown on irrigated land in the Darwin area.

Tourism is rapidly developing and has replaced cattle as the Territory's second most important industry. The presence of Kakadu National Park and Ayers Rock within the Territory's borders help to make it a very popular destination. These features are dealt with in the section on 'Seven Things Not to Miss' but there are other places of interest within the state which deserve a visit. Unfortunately, its size and the locations of popular features make getting around a real problem. Darwin and Alice Springs may both be used as centres for visiting these areas, one can get buses between the two and from them organised trips to places of interest. Having your own car though, especially in the Darwin – Katherine – Kakadu triangle and immediately around Alice Springs is a definite advantage. Car hire in these areas would probably work out cheaper than taking a series of organised bus trips, with the exception of the 450 km journey to Ayers Rock.

There are few towns of any size in the Northern Territory other than Darwin. Alice Springs (1,500 km south of Darwin) is the only other major centre. It has a population of over 20,000 and is important as a tourist base and supply centre for the settlements and stations of the outback. Alice Springs disappoints many people – it is very modern, complete with shopping centres and a pedestrianised mall (Todd Street). Work in the tourist trade may be possible here – there is a large number of hotels and motels. Worth seeing are the Royal Flying Doctor Base, on Stuart Terrace, and the Old Telegraph Station (2 km north of the city centre).

Other towns of the Northern Territory are Katherine (population 4,600) and Tennant Creek (population 2,300). These are important as wayside stops for travellers on the Stuart Highway (the 'Track' which leads eventually to Adelaide) and as supply centres for the remote cattle stations of the outback. They are far closer to the image of a dusty outback town popularised in Shute's *A Town like Alice* than clean, modern Alice Springs itself.

Canberra and the Australian Capital Territory

With an area of 2,359 km^2 and a population of about 265,000 the Australian Capital Territory is of interest to the tourist only as the site of the national capital. It is not the kind of place you would choose to settle in, and while it has pretty countryside and some nice bushwalks, there are other more spectacular places in Australia. Sixty per cent of all wage-earners living in Canberra are employed by government agencies or departments, so it is very much a civil service town.

Canberra is 320 km south-west of Sydney and 655 km north-west of Melbourne, centred around the man-made Lake Burley Griffin. This lake divides the city into two sections. One side of the lake is principally residential, the other (the south side) mostly devoted to business and administrative offices. This modern design makes for a very tidy, orderly city, with wide boulevards and rather inhuman proportions.

The scale of Canberra makes it daunting to walk around. Outside the city there are three independent satellite towns, Belconnen, Woden and Tuggeranong. Sixteen kilometres west of Canberra is the Australian National University's Stromlo Observatory. Containing a huge telescope and photographic exhibition it is of interest to the astronomy buff. Tidbinbilla, 40 km north-west has a space-tracking station, The Canberra Space Centre, which is also open to the public. There is a nature reserve nearby which has popular barbecue facilities and bushwalks.

The city is not exactly famous for its nightlife and almost closes entirely on public holidays. It did experience rapid growth, however, during the 1960s and early 1970s and as a result has a large young population. It is also the home of the Australian National University. These factors may make Canberra a more lively place in future, as it overcomes its artificial beginnings.

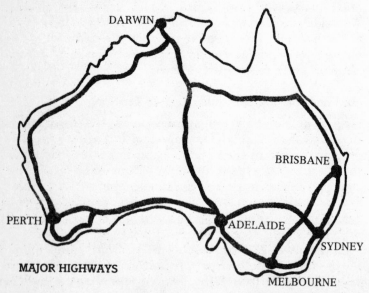

MAJOR HIGHWAYS

11 Going Walkabout – Holidays and Travel

Australia is made for holidays. The traveller is well catered for and there are thousands of unique and beautiful things to see. If you are migrating, try to travel a bit before you get bogged down in work and other commitments. If that is impossible, fix a definite holiday time within your first six months. You will appreciate a break from the pressures of settling into a new life, and learn a lot about your adoptive country. It is possible to live for years in a city and never see a 'roo or a snake or get any idea of the vastness of the outback – all the things for which Australia is famous. A good plan for those on working-holiday visas is to work for a longish period, save, travel, and spend it all, then repeat the process, working somewhere else. To stay in one place is definitely not the aim of a working-holiday. Anyway, it is a shame to miss the experiences this country has to offer.

Tourism is Australia's biggest single industry and one of its fastest growth areas. In 1984 it contributed 4.8% of the gross domestic product and directly or indirectly provided over 350,000 jobs. In that year over 1 million tourists visited Australia and spent about $1,400 million. Figures have shot up since then, with intensive marketing campaigns at home and abroad, especially in Japan and America. Well-known figures such as Barry Humphreys and Paul Hogan appear in television ads in Australia and overseas, and the States rival each other in their chauvinistic slogans. All Australians are exhorted to 'Smile and say G'day' to the moneyspending tourists.

Types of Holiday

The problem with zipping from city to city, airport to airport and from one tourist magnet to another is missing all the bits in the middle. The strange experiences you have, the people you meet on the road, the glimpses of wild animals, the strange places you end up in and – most of all – the sense of covering distance, make travelling and holidaying in

Australia unique. If you are short of time, it would be better to limit yourself to one area and travel overland rather than take an over-ambitious bunny-hopping round trip. It is less exhausting, cheaper and gives you a better feel for the true nature of the country. Use your judgement though. Obviously, some parts are tiresome to travel through, while others have great variety. Tasmania's compactness and scenic variety, for example, are what make it a good holiday spot.

By far the best way to go in Australia is to camp. Having your own transport and accommodation and cooking for yourself make for a very cheap holiday. In addition, you are close to the natural world and get to see more wildlife than you ever would in a hotel or hostel. Wombats, possums, wallabies, bandicoots, emus and dingoes will come to visit, depending on where you are. Of course, camping in Australia in summer is far different to camping in Ireland. Your worst enemy, the weather, is turned into your best friend.

The next-best thing to camping is using youth hostels, which are numerous and well-located in places of interest. If you are travelling in a group, on-site vans in caravan parks are also quite a good option. Holiday flats are useful, especially if you intend to live in a resort area for some time. Hotels and motels provide reasonable accommodation, but are expensive and rather limiting.

Australia is very much geared to adventurous outdoor holidays. Even in beach resorts, people spend more time snorkelling, wind-surfing and paragliding than they do lazing on the beach. Try bushwalking and outdoor pursuits and visit as many national parks as you can. They have excellent facilities, often free camp-grounds, information centres and ranger-guided walks. The whole idea is to get out of the cities and enjoy the wide-open spaces – they are Australia's best asset.

Information
There are three main sources of tourist information: guide books, tourist offices, and agencies such as The National Trust and The National Parks and Wildlife Service. A large number of guide books is available in Australia, from general guides to the whole country to those dealing with specialised interests such as wineries, wildflower areas or bushwalking. Try to limit yourself to one good general guide to take with you and

use local tourist information. Research as much as you can before you take off on holiday – it is terrible to miss things out of ignorance of their existence. Some guide books are suggested in the Books About Australia Section. Australians also love glossy photographic books and these are available for every area. Lovely to look at before you go, or to buy as a souvenir, they are too heavy and cumbersome to cart around.

Tourist information is free, for the most part. Before you leave Ireland you can write to the Australian Tourist Commission, the organisation which provides information for potential visitors. Its material is distributed overseas only and they have nothing to do with tourism within the country. Its London address may be found in the Useful Addresses section.

Tourist promotion within Australia is handled by State government bureaux. They each have offices in most capital cities, a head office in the State capital, and numerous local offices in towns or places of interest. The local offices may have specialised information on the local area, unavailable elsewhere, so make a point of visiting them. State offices provide reservation services for transport, special tours and accommodation and colourful guides and leaflets, good maps and quantities of information.

The National Parks and Wildlife Service has information offices in each city and often in the National Parks themselves. Addresses for the city offices may be found in the Useful Addresses section.

The National Trust is very similar to the British organisation. Dedicated to preserving historic buildings, they provide information and walking-tour guides of main towns, usually free. Membership of the trust is a good idea if you are going to be in Australia for any length of time, as it gives you free entry to their properties, their magazine, and better access to information. Addresses of State offices may be found in the Useful Addresses section.

How to go

When deciding whether to fly, take a bus or train, or drive yourself, the most important factor must be your time – or lack of it. Most of us from a small country totally under-estimate the distances and time taken to travel in Australia – we just are not used to reading maps of that scale.

Flying

The chief advantage of flying is its speed, particularly if you would otherwise be crawling over very boring terrain. You also have great comfort, aerial views and always some kind of snack – unless it is a terribly short flight. Alcoholic drink is usually extra on internal flights.

Flying is expensive, and there seems to be little true price competition. East-West Airlines is a less expensive company, but it doesn't have the range of destinations of the big two. Cheapest ways to go are on Airpasses, covering a number of destinations, or Super Saver/Standby fares. Discounts are available for tourists who have recently arrived in the country and have an onward ticket. These are not well advertised, so ask.

The disadvantages of flying include the cost and hassle of getting to and from airports, missing out on things at ground level and most of all, the price of the tickets.

Overland travel

Overland travel costs are surprisingly similar, whatever means you choose, when everything – fuel, food on the way, accommodation if you need it, books and magazines to kill the boredom, spares and emergency precautions if driving – is taken into consideration. The major exception to this is express bus travel, which is definitely the cheapest means of getting around.

Dots on maps

One peculiarity of road travel in Australia is that places marked on maps may not exist at all. While in Ireland a dot on a map usually means something worth stopping and look-ing at, in Australia the dot can be just a dot and no more. If you are lucky there may be a roadhouse; often there is nothing. Blink and it is gone. Don't bother going back to look, for example, for Shannon River in south-east WA, it is not there.

Bus travel

This is relatively very cheap. Best bet of all is to buy a ticket for your ultimate destination, rather than a pass or tickets for lots of intermediate short journeys. Most companies will allow you to break off and resume your journey without time limitations. The only difficulty here is timetable. Many express services travel through the night and may miss out on, or simply not stop at, intermediate points. You must also always reconfirm and reserve your onward journey, so allow a certain time flexibility – a bus with a spare seat may be harder to come by from Kalgoorlie than from a major city.

The major companies offer many different passes and discounts – including 10% less for those with International Student Identity Cards or Australian Youth Hostel Association (AYHA) Cards. Research prices carefully – and the limitations of time and timetable on inclusive passes – before buying. For example, a straightforward ticket from Perth to Sydney will allow you to stop at Adelaide, Melbourne and Canberra, and many other places in between, without time restrictions, whereas a pass (Koala Pass, Eagle Pass etc) provides unlimited kilometres within a certain period, at a far higher price. You've got to remember there's only so much ground you can cover in 15, 30 or 60 days – the danger with most bus passes is over-ambition.

Long-distance bus travel is surprisingly comfortable. It is worth paying a bit extra for a comfortable coach: DeLuxe Bus Company's Superdeckers are particularly nice, with good reclining seats, video, cold drinking water, toilet and a great view from the top deck. If time isn't a problem, bus is the cheapest way to go.

Train travel
There is nothing quite like a good long train trip. But trains in Australia are expensive. Tickets cost from 30% to 50% more than a bus would for the same journey. If you already own a car, taking a train or driving yourself would require similar amounts of money.

Trains are the slowest overland transport. Timetabling and frequency are also poor because of the great distances and small number of passengers on most express services. If you want to break your journey, your ticket will probably allow you to, but it can mean (as between Sydney and Brisbane) getting off the train and picking up the onward train in the middle of the night. Train travel has advantages though, apart from the sheer joy of watching the countryside roll slowly by. You are likely to meet more Australians and fewer tourists than on buses. Because they get discounts, most of your fellow passengers will be railway workers or pensioners. The bar is a good place for making friends and whiling away the time with card games, chess and draughts.

The trains are comfortable, with a bar, dining carriage, showers and sleepers for most long journeys. Sleepers are expensive ($40 to $60 on top of your ticket), but the luxury is worth it if you can afford it. Most ordinary carriage seats are less comfortable for sitting or sleeping on than those on buses. Food and drink are a little more expensive than usual, but not exorbitant.

There are some really famous train journeys in Australia and if you enjoy rail travel, it is worth experiencing at least one long trip – perhaps the Ghan from Alice Springs to Adelaide, the Sunlander from Brisbane to Cairns, or the Indian Pacific right across the continent.

Car travel

The advantages of driving yourself are obvious – you are your own boss, can see everything, take your own time and detour as much as you like. Holidaying in your own car is in many ways the ideal way to go, but there are disadvantages. First, it is more expensive than the bus, especially as you are likely to be in a cheap second-hand car that drinks petrol. You will also find it slow and tiring. For most long journeys you will need at least two drivers in the car. Finally, the danger of driving at night, the precautions and spares you must take before going off into the outback, and the high prices charged for food and drink in most roadhouses mean that car travel is a holiday in itself as regards cost, rather than a means of getting from one place to another for your holiday to begin. If you own a car anyway, or can afford to hire one, driving is the most interesting way to go. It is definitely not as cheap or as easy as travelling by bus. For more information on the need for a car and the problems of hiring or buying one, see the section on vehicles.

Seven things not to miss

This is a short list of some things that make Australia a great holiday continent. Most are well-known tourist destinations and some, at least, you should get to while in Australia – not because everyone else goes to them, but because they are worth visiting in their own right. It is a highly personal list of top spots, in no way comprehensive. You will be able to add many more.

Sydney Opera House (Bennelong Point, Sydney, New South Wales).
It is difficult to explain the powerful attraction of this building, or why so many people make the pilgrimage to stand on its steps every year. It appears surprisingly small when you see it first – perhaps because you anticipate that shape made familiar by so many photos and postcards. Eventually the roof structure starts to catch the eye from all vantage points on the harbour.

As well as walking around it, preferably in sunshine when the millions of tiny tiles catch the light from different angles, venture inside. Guided tours, filled with statistics, are run every day. Try to catch a performance in one of its theatres or concert hall instead of simply taking a tour. The scale and grandeur of the auditoria are worth experiencing. You can often get half-price tickets, those still unsold on the day of the performance, at the Half-Tix booth on Martin Place, beside the tourist information stand. Seven dollars or so to experience the National Symphony Orchestra in full flight in the concert hall is a real bargain. The atmosphere in this venue is very sophisticated, people dress up, and champagne is available to be sipped on a balcony over the harbour at the interval.

There is a waterside snack bar at the rear of the building, where you can dine and drink, in the company of lots of very greedy seagulls – watch your dinner! This spot is specially popular on Sunday mornings, when bands play. The shop in the Opera House has particularly nice, relatively cheap souvenirs, many of which are unavailable elsewhere.

The Great Barrier Reef (Queensland).
Everyone has heard of the 2,000 km long belt of coral reefs and islands in north-eastern Queensland that makes up the

Great Barrier Reef. You have to see some of its 400 varieties of coral, 10,000 species of sponges, 4,000 species of molluscs and more than 1,500 species of brightly coloured tropical fish. You can swim round it, scuba-dive, walk over it, (watch out for the stone-fish) take a glass-bottomed boat over it or look at it through the windows of an underwater observatory. It is the world's largest marine conservation reserve (345,000 km^2), most of its islands are also national parks. The cheapest place to reach it from is probably Cairns, which offers all sorts of day trips to more accessible reefs and islands.

Kakadu National Park (Northern Territory).
This has to be the most exciting of Australia's wonderful national parks. It was placed on the United Nations World Heritage list as a place to be preserved for future generations on the basis of its scenic beauty, cultural significance and ecological value. It is in a remote area, 220 km east of Darwin, but has been recently developed to be relatively easily accessible with surfaced roads, two motels and several free campgrounds. Go there and learn about its animals, see the fantastic birds, see crocodiles undisturbed in the wild and look at some of the best examples of Aboriginal art in Australia.

Lake St Clair – Cradle Mountain (Tasmania).
This is a mountainous national park which contains a world-famous walking trail; 85 km long, it can be attempted if you are reasonably fit and adventurous, taking you through five days of some of the most beautiful scenery in the world. It is quite difficult terrain, often wet and boggy underfoot, so the Overland Track should be approached with caution. There are numerous short bushwalks in the area too, suitable for the more fainthearted and it is easily accessible by car and bus from either end.

Make a point of getting there, preferably to camp, and see the tamed wallabies and possums that frequent the camping grounds, take a walk and enjoy the misty, mountain scenery including the highest mountain in Tasmania, Mount Ossa (1,617 metres) and the deepest natural freshwater lake in Australia, Lake St Clair. If you are very lucky, you may see a platypus. There is also a lodge at the Cradle Mountain end of the Park with a nocturnal window, go there and see possums, mountain cats and the famed Tasmanian Devil fighting over the sliced pan the lodge leaves out for them. This 126,205 hectare national park is really challenging and would appeal especially to out-door types who enjoy hard-won pleasures.

Kuranda Scenic Railway (Cairns, Far North Queensland).
This little train trip, 34 km long, is a real adventure. You climb through the mountains between Cairns and the Atherton tableland, passing through 15 tunnels, deep gorges, and over sheer precipices, in a little rattling train on a twisting narrow-gauge track. Anyone who regrets being too young to have experienced the renowned narrow-gauge railways of Ireland's west coast has here the chance to try something which must be similar, if on another continent in another hemisphere. High point of the journey is crossing the bridge over the spectacular Barron Falls: on one side a Niagarous waterfall, on the other a sheer drop to the gorge below. Patrick Kavanagh, eat your heart out.

The trip takes about two hours, and brings you to Kuranda, a pretty town with a railway station as green as any fernery in the Botanical Gardens. Here you can visit the Butterfly Sanctuary, a Nocturnal House (watch the sugar gliders making their gravity-defying leaps from tree to tree) and numerous art galleries, craft shops and other tourist attractions. There is also a market on Sunday and Wednesday mornings.

Undeniably touristy, the trip, with its views of cane fields, tropical vegetation and the sea around Cairns, from an antique train and with an interesting destination, is well worth taking.

Ayers Rock [Uluru] (Yulara, Northern Territory).
This great red rock, the largest monolith in the world, has a definite air of mystery. Unfortunately its popularity with tourists, despite its relative remoteness, makes the path to its summit like a busy street. The walking track around its base (10 km long, an easy four hours) provides a chance to get away from the crowds and appreciate the rock's special atmosphere.

It is of tremendous spiritual significance to the Aboriginal tribes of the area, who fought for years to recover it from the tourist trade. The rather unsatisfactory solution finally reached in 1985 was the transfer of the free-hold title to an

Aboriginal Land Trust, who in turn lease it back to the Federal government. Some especially important sacred sites have been fenced off and tourists are requested not to disturb them. Still, it's a poor solution in that the Aboriginals get lots of money, but not their rock back, and the tourist trade goes on.

Ayers Rock is 335 metres high above the open plain around it, 3.6 km long and 2.5 km wide. Every day hundreds of tourists climb up its sheer slopes to the summit. The view from the top is fantastic, but the ascent is quite nerveracking. It's very surprising more people don't slip, or die of heart attacks, than the present statistic of a couple of deaths every year.

Made of a conglomerate of compacted gravel and boulders, and eroded into a smooth surface with many hollows by wind-driven sand, its red colour is part of its fascination. Ayers Rock would not be the same if it were grey, or brown. Part of the Great Western Plateau, like Mount Lofty above Adelaide and the Stirling and Kimberley Ranges, it is of the preCambrian era, somewhere between 2,600 and 600 million years old. There are neighbouring rocks of similar vintage, Mount Connor and the Olgas, which are equally fascinating. All are located in the 1,325 km^2 of desert that make up Uluru National Park. It is 463 km from Alice Springs and can only be visited from Yulara, the resort centre specially built for the purpose.

Yulara was specially designed to blend into the scenery and replaced the jumble of hotels and campsites that had grown up around Ayers Rock's base. 450 km from Alice Springs it is totally self-contained and can accommodate 5,000 visitors with 800 resident service personnel. It has a huge campsite and two expensive hotels. There is also the Ayers Rock Lodge, the only place offering hostel-type accommodation. It gets heavily booked and is usually filled to capacity every night – if you are going to Ayers Rock, book this first. Many bus companies operate packages from Alice Springs to Yulara and Ayers Rock. These are the cheapest option, but make one feel horribly sheep-like. All leave at the same time, and visit the same points of interest. You are shepherded on and off the buses like clockwork – climb the rock at 8.00 am, tour of the base at 11.30, sunset photos at

6.30 etc., etc. Try to take an extra day – easily arranged with most companies – to explore on your own and avail of the excellent ranger-guided walks at its base (far better than those of some ill-informed couriers with private bus companies). You should also see the Aboriginals' video about the rock and what it means to them – on display in Yulara Information Centre and at the rangers' station 1.5 km from its base. It is called *Uluru, an Angangu Story*.

The Pinnacles Desert (near Cervantes, Western Australia).
In the Nambung National Park, 260 km north of Perth, is a strange landscape of limestone pillars. They are the product of millions of years of erosion and consist of hundreds of columns, located in a sandy desert. Some are tiny, sticking out of the sand, others are tall and strangely phallic. Their shape and sheer quantity make a marvellous sight, particularly as the light goes down and they cast long shadows. Old legends of strange petrified armies come to mind as your imagination runs riot.

Cervantes is the base for seeing the Pinnacles, you can get bus trips from Perth, or go by private car. The access road is extremely rough and difficult to negotiate without a four-wheel drive vehicle. This little-known area is one of Australia's natural wonders, and possibly the strangest.

Six things to avoid

Australia has more than its share of dangerous, and even deadly, animals. Being unused to them at home, some Irish people get absolutely paranoid whenever they step outside their front doors. This is taking things too far, but it is only sensible to enquire about the dangers and to pay careful attention to advice from the locals. People who fail to do this and swim in crocodile infested areas or shove their hands under logs where snakes may live, get scant sympathy.

Stonefish
This member of the family *Synanceidae* is believed to be the most venomous fish in the world. Along its back are 13 spines, each of which contains two venom glands. Their venom causes intense pain and swelling and can attack the nervous system, leading, in extreme cases, to paralysis and death. They are found in estuaries and bays of eastern Australia.

Box jellyfish or sea-wasp
From late November to March these jellyfish are common in
the sea off northern Australia. They are transparent and
nearly impossible to see in the water, with stinging tentacles
stretching behind them. Any sting will cause extreme pain
and scarring. A major sting may kill either directly or by
causing the person to pass out and drown. During the season,
do not swim in the sea except in specially netted areas.
Observe the warning signs and ask local advice.

Sharks
Sharks of many species inhabit the waters around Australia.
Most major swimming areas have nets extended out to sea,
at right angles to the beach, to prevent sharks from cruising
along the beach as they like to do. Pay attention to local warn-
ings and do not swim near fish processing plants or in other
places where blood and offal are discharged into the sea.

Crocodiles
You saw the film. . . Australia has two species of crocodile:
the smaller freshwater, or Johnston's Crocodile, which is
harmless to man in most circumstances and the larger, more
aggressive and far more dangerous Estuarine Crocodile.
Estuarine Crocodiles can be found quite far up rivers, in land-
locked billabongs, and in the sea at night as they move from
creek to creek. They are found from Maryborough in Queensland to the Kimberley ranges in WA. Do not camp on river
banks, clean fish at the water's edge or swim in these areas
unless you are certain it is safe. If you see a croc and are
unsure of which species it is, keep well clear. A saltie, as
Estuarine Crocodiles are also known, can outrun you over
short stretches. They cannot climb trees, fortunately, but they
can jump bloody high.

Spiders
While all spiders have a venom for killing their prey, Australia
has several species capable of killing a human. The funnel-
webs, Sydney funnel-web and tree funnel-web, are found
under rocks and tree roots within a 200 km radius of Sydney,
and in tree trunks in NSW and Queensland respectively. Both
are capable of killing a human adult. The Redback is found
under stones, rubbish and houses throughout Australia and

may kill an adult. There are antivenoms available for the bites of these spiders, but don't bank on that. Treat all spiders with respect and use a stick if you want to poke around in fallen leaves. The black house spider's bite can also cause great pain.

Snakes

Australia has 110 species of snake, of which at least 28 are dangerously venomous. Some of them are among the most deadly snakes in the world. Treat any snake you see with great care and keep well away from it. In general, snakes will flee from the footfalls of an approaching human, but beware of coming on them by surprise. Observe simple common sense rules, like not running through long grass in thongs and not shoving your hand under rocks or logs, and you should be right.

12 History of Australia – The First 45 Million Years

45 million years ago: Australia separated from Asia and Antarctica. Animals and birds were isolated from the rest of the world and began to develop unique Australian forms, including giant kangaroos and wombats.

2 million years ago: Last Ice Age began, while Australia was home to huge animals and birds.

About 40,000 years ago: Aboriginal people began arriving in Australia from south-east Asia.

15,000 years ago: The huge animals began to die out. Some species, like the echidna and wombat survived in a smaller form. Others, like the donkey-sized wombat and the 10-foot tall kangaroo disappeared.

Sixth century BC: Some evidence of contact with Australia by Chinese explorers.

1616: Dutchman Dirck Hartog lands at Shark Bay, Western Australia.

1642: Dutch sailor Abel Tasman discovers and maps south of Tasmania, naming the island Van Diemen's Land.

1669-70: William Dampier explores the coast of WA and decides it is not fit for human habitation.

1770: Captain James Cook explores the east coast of Australia and proclaims it a British possession to be called New South Wales.

1786: Seven years after botanist Joseph Banks recommended the establishment of a penal settlement in Australia, the British Parliament is told '. . . His majesty has thought it advisable to fix upon Botany Bay. . .'

1788: First Fleet, under Captain Arthur Phillip, arrives and Phillip decides on Sydney Cove as a better site for the colony. He hoists the British flag there on 26 January. In May, the first violence between white settlers and Aborigines takes place when two Aborigines are killed at Rushcutters Bay.

1789: First play, *The Recruiting Officer*, put on by convicts for the King's birthday.

1790: Famine hits the colony and rations are cut. The Second Fleet leaves England with 1,006 convicts, of whom over a quarter die on the way.

1792: First assisted immigration brings three farmers, a gardener, a baker, a millwright and two women with four children. The use of rum as a currency begins.

1796: First commercially brewed beer, first commercial theatre.

1797: Thirteen Merino sheep imported and coalmining begins near the present site of Newcastle, NSW.

1800: The first taxes in Australia, on spirits, wine and beer are used to build a jail.

1802: Matthew Flinders circumnavigates Australia in the *Investigator.* First book, *New South Wales General Standing Orders* published in Sydney.

1803: First newspaper is *The Sydney Gazette and NSW Advertiser.* Van Diemen's Land settled by a small group of soldiers and convicts.

1804: Fifty Aborigines shot in Van Diemen's Land. Three hundred Irish convicts rebel and riot at Castle Hill then march on Parramatta. Troops kill nine, the six leaders are hanged.

1806: Captain William Bligh, having survived mutiny on the *Bounty* arrives as governor and tries to put down the rum trade.

1808: In the 'rum rebellion', the NSW Corps depose Bligh because he tried to ban the use of rum as currency, a trade which they monopolise.

1813: John Macarthur sells his first shipment of wool in London.

1814: Flinders publishes *A Voyage to Terra Australis* in which he pushes the name 'Australia' instead of 'New Holland', as the continent was then known.

1819: There are 26,026 people in NSW, 38% of them convicts. Van Diemen's Land has 4,270 people, 47% of them convicts.

1823: Gold is discovered at Fish River, near Bathurst. Five-member advisory Legislative Council appointed.

1825: Van Diemen's Land becomes a separate colony. First settlement of Western Australia, at Albany.

1826: Government campaign against the Aborigines in Van Diemen's Land begins, which leads to a 3,000-man effort to beat them into the natural prison of the Tasman Peninsula. This fails.

1829: Captain Stirling, in the *Parmelia*, brings 69 settlers from England to establish the Swan River Colony, now Perth.

1831: The *Sydney Herald* is established and becomes the colony's leading newspaper. It became the *Sydney Morning Herald* twelve years later.

1832: Large-scale assisted immigration began. Over the next 37 years, 339,000 British people arrived in Australia.

1834: British pass an Act to set up South Australia under the rational humanistic plan drafted by Wakefield. Captain Stirling kills 80 Aborigines at the 'battle' of Pinjarra in reprisal for the death of a white man.

1837: Melbourne named and first overland mail service between Sydney and Melbourne established. Molesworth Committee investigated the use of transportation of criminals. Its report, the next year, condemned transportation but did not recommend its immediate abolition.

1839: Governor of NSW given control of New Zealand. *HMS Beagle* discovers and names Port Darwin in honour of the scientist. When evolutionary theory becomes controversial Darwin is renamed Palmerston, only to revert to Darwin in 1911. Major WD Mercer imports the first pack of fox hounds. Foxes and deer went on to become major pests.

1840: First camels imported. Transportation abolished for NSW.

1841: Edward John Eyre completed first crossing of the continent from east to west, despite the killing of his companion, John Baxter, by Aborigines.

1842: NSW's Legislative Council enlarged and Melbourne City Council established.

1846: First swimming championship held at the Domain Baths in Sydney.

1848: Ludwig Leichhardt tries to cross the continent from east to west but disappears without trace. Edmund Kennedy's expedition in Queensland ended in disaster. He was speared to death in sight of his goal and only two of the eight-man group survived.

1850: First convicts arrive in WA while other States agitate for an end to transportation. University of Sydney is set up.

1851: Gold rushes begin in the eastern States. There were 10,000 men on the NSW diggings, but when the Bendigo field opened Victoria overtook NSW as the main gold State. NSW and Victoria separated.

1854: First telegraph opened. First steam train runs. Diggers rebel at Eureka Stockade under the leadership of Peter Lalor.

1855: Van Diemen's Land renamed Tasmania. Responsible government granted to NSW, Tasmania and Victoria. South Australia got it in 1857, but WA did not get it until 1890.

1856: Victoria introduces first secret ballot in the world. NSW plays Victoria in the first inter-colony cricket match.

1858: Population goes above one million. Melbourne Grammar and Scotch College play the first game of what is to become Australian Rules football with 40-man teams and goals half a mile apart.

1859: Queensland separated from NSW and gets responsible government. Thomas Austin imports 72 partridges and 24 rabbits. By 1865, he is believed to have killed 20,000 rabbits on his property. Other Australian farmers have had to do the same ever since.

1861: Robert O'Hara Burke and William John Wills died in the desert when they missed the rest of their expedition party by hours. Three thousand miners attack Chinese miners at Lambing Flat and Chinese immigration to NSW is curtailed as a result.

1862: Queensland starts to grow sugar commercially. John McDouall Stuart crosses the continent from south to north, providing the route for the overland telegraph that is to link

Australia and Europe ten years later.

1868: Transportation ended when the last convict ship reached WA. An Aboriginal cricket team tours England, the first touring Australian team. Maria Ann Smith accidentally invents the 'Granny Smith' apple.

1873: William Gosse discovers the biggest rock in the world, Ayers Rock, and names it after the South Australian Governor, Sir Henry Ayers.

1876: Truganini, the last full-blooded Tasmanian Aboriginal dies in Hobart at 73 and her body is displayed in the Tasmanian Museum for over 40 years.

1877: Population passes two million. First commercial telephone. First Test cricket match. Adelaide and Perth connected by telegraph.

1879: First successful shipment of frozen meat to Britain. Royal National Park is established, the first in Australia and the second in the world.

1880: First census finds 2.25 million people, not counting Aborigines.

1883: Julia Balla Guerin becomes the first woman to graduate from an Australian university. Moves towards federation of the States.

1886: William Guthrie Spence forms the Amalgamated Shearers' Union to fight wage-cutting by large farmers. It gained 16,000 members within a year.

1888: WM Foster started his brewery in Victoria and the next year launched Foster's Lager on the world. Queenland and NSW get their first rail link. First successful mechanical shearing of sheep.

1891: The first Labor Party is formed.

1894: Beginning of an eight-year drought which was to kill 36 million sheep. South Australia becomes first colony to give women the vote.

1896: Victoria introduces minimum wage. First moving pictures in Australia shown in Melbourne.

1899: Australia begins sending the first of 16,000 troops to the Boer War. In all, 251 men were killed and 267 died from disease during the campaign.

1900: The population of Sydney and Melbourne approached half a million. On 9 July Queen Victoria gives her assent to the Commonwealth of Australia Constitution Act. Bubonic plague breaks out in Sydney. Aboriginal brothers Jimmy and Joe Governor kill seven whites, the incident that was the basis for the book *The Chant of Jimmy Blacksmith* by Thomas Keneally.

1901: Australia federated on 1 January. Australian flag selected. It has the Union Jack, a six-pointed star below to symbolise the States and the Southern Cross on a blue ground. Duke of York opens first national Parliament in Melbourne. Aborigines excluded from census and citizenship.

1904: Commonwealth Court of Conciliation and Arbitration is established to deal with industrial disputes and wage claims. WA builds a 1,800-kilometre fence from Port Hedland in the north to Esperance in the south to keep rabbits out. They got through.

1906: What was Australia's, and is claimed to be the world's, first feature film, *The Story of the Kelly Gang* is made by Millard Johnson and William Gibson. Bondi Surf Life Saving Club is formed.

1907: Australia, with Canada and New Zealand, gets Dominion Status. Britain consults them about foreign policy but they cannot make independent decisions. Principle of basic wage established. Rugby League begins in NSW.

1909: Canberra chosen as site for national capital after Yass, Tumur, Bamabala, Dalgety and Albury are considered.

1911: Royal Australian Navy established. First Federal census finds 4,455,005 non-Aboriginal people in Australia. The transcontinental railway line, which had been used to entice WA into federation, is started.

1912: American architect Walter Burley Griffin designs Canberra.

1914: Australia enters the First World War on the side of Britain. Australian and New Zealand Army Corps (ANZAC) is set up. The first (volunteer) Australian Imperial Force of

20,000 men is raised and sails for Egypt.

1915: First Commonwealth income tax is introduced. Allied troops, including ANZACs, land at Gallipoli. Although Australia lost 7,600 men and 19,000 were wounded in a futile campaign, this is widely seen as the coming of age of Australia. A Hawaiian, Duke Kahanamoku, demonstrates surfing on a 36-kilogram pine board.

1916: Returned Sailors', Soldiers' and Airmen's League (now the RSL) is founded. After Australians distinguish themselves but lose men heavily in the slaughter of the Somme, a referendum is held on the introduction of conscription and narrowly defeated.

1917: South Australia bans the teaching of German. The Trans-Australia Railway opens from Port Augusta to Kalgoorlie, but because of differing gauges passengers must change trains three times between Sydney and Perth. A second conscription referendum is heavily defeated.

1918: War ends. Of the 329,000 Australians, all volunteers, who have served overseas, 59,330 have been killed and 151,171 wounded. Australian population reaches five million.

1919: Australia is a founding member of the League of Nations. An Influenza epidemic kills over 11,000. First public broadcast. Daisy May Bates, self-taught welfare worker and anthropologist, sets up the camp at Ooldea where she is to tend Aborigines until 1935.

1920: Queensland and Northern Territory Aerial Services (QANTAS) is formed.

1921: Edith Cowan becomes first woman elected to an Australian Parliament, in WA.

1923: Vegemite is invented by C P Callister.

1924: Sugar and koala skins exported. Voting in Federal elections becomes compulsory.

1925: The Prickly Pear Board, set up five years earlier, sets loose 30,000 caterpillar eggs to attack the weed and within ten years most of the plants have been exterminated.

1926: Western Australia begins agitating to leave the Commonwealth.

1927: Australasian (now Australian) Council of Trade Unions established. Federal Parliament meets for the first time in Canberra.

1928: Flying doctor service set up by the Rev John Flynn. Charles Kingsford Smith and Charles Ulm make the first trans-Pacific flight in nine days.

1929: James Joyce's *Ulysses* banned.

1930: Harold Lasseter dies in the central desert searching for a spectacular reef of gold he believes exists.

1932: Sydney Harbour Bridge opened after a delay when F de Groot galloped his horse to the ribbon and slashed it before the Premier could do so. He got 2,500 letters of congratulation.

1933: WA votes by a large majority to leave the Commonwealth, but the British tell it that all Australia must vote to allow any State to leave. Town of Stuart renamed Alice Springs after Lady Alice Todd, wife of the Superintendent of Telegraphs for South Australia.

1934: Sugar growers imported the cane toad to control the grey-backed beetle. The poisonous toad failed to kill the beetle and went on to become a major pest.

1937: Federal and State governments agree on an enforced policy of assimilation for Aborigines into white society.

1938: One hundred and eighty people rescued from the sea at Bondi Beach on a single day.

1939: Forty-five minutes after Britain, Australia declares war on Germany. Conscription for military service at home introduced. First sliced bread.

1941: Australians fight in North Africa, Greece, Syria and Crete. War declared on Japan.

1942: Japanese make the first of 50 bombing raids on Darwin that are to kill 233 people. Over 15,000 Australians captured by Japanese after fall of Singapore. Many of them later starved or were worked to death by their captors. The battles of Coral Sea, Midway and the Kokoda Trail begin to halt the Japanese advance.

1943: Conscription for overseas military service. Post

between Australia and Britain sent on microfilm. PAYE tax starts.

1944: Liberal Party formed. Japanese POWs break out of Cowra camp and 232 are killed. Meat rationed.

1945: War ends with 33,552 Australians killed out of a total enlistment of 926,000 men and 63,100 women.

1946: First celebration of Australia Day.

1947: Commonwealth buys QANTAS. Australia agrees to accept displaced Europeans and an estimated 250,000 arrive in the late 1940s and early 1950s.

1949: Australians became Austalian citizens, but still used British passports.

1950: Communist Party banned. Australia enters Korean war. Myxomatosis introduced to kill rabbits. It worked.

1951: Chiko Roll invented. ANZUS defence alliance entered with New Zealand and the United States, marking a shift from dependence on Britain in defence matters.

1952: First British atomic bomb exploded on Monte Bello islands off coast of WA.

1953: Britain explodes several atomic bombs at Woomera, South Australia. Not all Aborigines are removed from the area first.

1956: Melbourne hosts Olympic Games. Television begins in Sydney. Edna Everage created.

1957: Australian Labor party split over communist influence. Joern Utzon designed Sydney Opera House.

1959: Population reaches ten million.

1962: First Australians sent to Vietnam. Aborigines get the right to vote in Federal elections in Queensland, WA and the Northern Territory.

1964: *The Australian*, published by Rupert Murdoch, became the first national newspaper.

1966: Australia gives up pounds and switches to the decimal dollar. US President Lyndon Johnson visits Australia and Prime Minister Harold Holt produces the slogan 'All the way with LBJ' as a sign of his enthusiasm. The first national servicemen are sent to Vietnam, bringing the number of Australians there to 4,500.

1967: Ronald Ryan, hanged in Melbourne, becomes the last man executed in Australia. By a 90.8% 'yes' vote, a referendum to end all forms of legal discrimination against Aborigines is carried. They are included in the census for the first time and the Constitution is amended to allow the Federal Government to legislate for them as well as the States.

1968: Commonwealth Council and Office of Aboriginal Affairs founded. It became a department in 1972. Australia's population reached twelve million.

1969: The principle of equal pay for women is established. Standard gauge railway finally completed from Sydney to Perth.

1970: The Indian Pacific train service inaugurated from Perth to Sydney, one of the great train journeys of the world. It contains the longest stretch of straight track in the world, 478 kilometres. Pope Paul VI tours Australia.

1971: Senator Neville Bonner became the first Aboriginal member of an Australian Parliament. Troops begin to leave Vietnam. Jack Mundey, leader of the Builders Laborers' Federation, used the term 'green ban' for the first time for his members' refusal to destroy landmarks and sites that they felt were significant.

1972: Under Gough Whitlam, the first Labor government in 23 years is elected. The new government recognised Communist China and withdrew the last Australian troops from Vietnam. The Gurindji Aboriginal tribe win limited legal rights to their traditional lands.

1973: Bob Hawke, president of the ACTU, elected unopposed as president of the Labor Party. Sydney Opera House completed after 16 years and $100 million compared with an original estimate of $7 million. Queen Elizabeth II opened it and the first production was Prokofiev's opera *War and Peace*. Patrick White wins Nobel Prize for literature with *The Eye of the Storm*.

1974: Woodward Report outlines the principles of Aboriginal land rights. *Advance Australia Fair* replaces *God Save the*

Queen as national anthem. On Christmas Day, Cyclone Tracy destroys Darwin, killing at least 50, causing the evacuation of 30,000 and necessitating the rebuilding of most of the city.

1975: Law against racial discrimination comes into force. Colour television introduced. Whitlam Labor Government dismissed by the Governor-General, Sir John Kerr.

1976: Family Court of Australia set up and the concept of no-fault divorce, based on one year's separation, is established. Aboriginal pastor Sir Douglas Nicholls becomes Governor of South Australia. *God Save the Queen* returns as national anthem.

1977: The country's worst rail disaster kills 80 at Granville in NSW. *The Sullivans* television series is sold to England, the first of thirty countries that buy it over the next five years.

1978: Northern Territory gains self-government, instead of being under South Australia. Menzies dies. Over the year, 47 battered vessels full of Vietnamese boat people arrived at Darwin.

1979: Australian diplomats ordered to leave Iran. The legal concept that Australia was an unoccupied land, without settled inhabitants or laws, at the time of the arrival of the British (which had been established in 1869) was challenged. The challenge failed.

1980: Bob Hawke enters Parliament. Azaria Chamberlain disappears at Ayers Rock. Her mother says she was taken by a dingo, a view accepted by the first inquest in 1981. The world's oldest fossil fish, 480 million years old, found near Alice Springs.

1981: Population reached 14.9 million. There were 159,600 Aborigines. The Pitjantjatjara tribal group won land rights in South Australia. Australia's own dictionary, *The Macquarie* is published. Rupert Murdoch buys the London *Times*.

1982: Unemployment reaches record levels. Controversy rages over the damming of the Franklin River in Tasmania. After a second inquest in 1981, Lindy Chamberlain is tried and found guilty of murdering her daughter and sentenced to life imprisonment.

1983: The 'Ash Wednesday' bushfires swept through Victoria and South Australia, killing 68. The Labor Party was elected to power and Bob Hawke became Prime Minister. His new minister for Sport, Recreation and Tourism caused a storm when he described Australia's favourite symbol, the koala, as 'a flea-ridden, piddling, stinking, scratching, rotten little thing'. Australia wins the America's Cup.

1984: *Advance Australia Fair* replaces *God Save the Queen* once again as national anthem. Hawke Government goes to the people and is returned with a reduced majority. Anti-nuclear protests bring 250,000 people onto the streets on Palm Sunday. Population reaches 15.45 million. The 'Bandido' and 'Commanchero' bikie gangs have a shoot-out in a pub car park in the Sydney suburb of Milperra, leaving six men and a girl of fourteen dead.

1985: John Howard takes over from Andrew Peacock as leader of the Federal Liberal Party. Lindy Chamberlain released from prison, three years into her sentence, after widespread disquiet and public agitation about the conviction. Adelaide hosts Australia's first Formula One Grand Prix. After a long and bitter campaign, Ayers Rock is handed over to Aboriginal owners who are to lease it perpetually to the Commonwealth.

1986: Australia's defence of the America's Cup begins off Fremantle, Perth's port, in Western Australia. Sir Joh Bjelke-Petersen defies the polls and wins another term as Premier of Queensland. Rupert Murdoch begins a battle to take over the *Herald* and *Weekly Times* group. With his victory in 1987, the number of major newspaper owners drops from three to two. Hawke Government brings down an austere budget.

1987: Bob Hawke wins an historic third term as Prime Minister, despite promises early in the year not to call an early election. His victory is helped by disarray in the opposition, caused by Sir Joh's entry to Federal politics, splitting the Liberal/National Party coalition. Australia loses the America's Cup to the San Diego Yacht Club. The Federal Government struggles with the State Governments of Tasmania and Queensland over conservation. Preparation for the 1988 bicentenary get into full swing, with events planned for all parts of the country. Bob Hawke visits Ireland. Meryl Streep is to star in *Evil Angels* the film of the Chamberlain case.

13 Useful Addresses

Accommodation

Sydney

Youth Hostels (about $7 a night in a dormitory) 28 Ross Street, Parramatta Road, Forest Lodge. Phone 692 0747
262 Glebe Point Road, Glebe.
YWCA (women and couples $13 for a bed in small dorm, twice that for single rooms) 5–11 Wentworth Avenue (corner of Liverpool Street, very central). Phone 264 2451. This has a good cheap cafeteria and lower rates for longer stays.

Private hostels

Kings Cross Backpackers Hostel, Victoria Street, Kings Cross. Phone 356 3232. (About $8 in a dorm, twice that for a room. Good for making work/travelling contacts, buying cars etc.)
Young Cross Country Travellers Centre, 25 Hughes Street, Kings Cross. Phone: 358 1143.

Hotels

Springfield Lodge, 9 Springfield Street, Kings Cross. Phone: 358 3222. ($20 single, $26 double, with discounts for week-long stays. Rooms have light cooking facilities (fridge, toaster, kettle) which makes eating a lot cheaper.
Pacific Coast Budget Accommodation, 400 Pitt Street, Phone: 211 5777
CB Private Hotel, Pitt Street. Phone: 211 5115
Both are in the city centre, with single rooms under $20.

Melbourne

Youth Hostels (about $8 for a dorm) 500 Abbotsford Street, North Melbourne. Phone: 328 2880.
76 Chapman Street, North Melbourne. Phone: 328 3595. (Close together, about three kilometres from the city centre. Tram 54, 57, 59 or 68 from the city.)
YWCA Family Hostel, 489 Elizabeth Street. Phone: 329 5188. Right in town, on the main street, very near terminals for airport and inter-city buses. It is expensive, $40 for a double,

but that includes en suite bathroom in a luxurious modern room.

Hotels

Victoria Hotel, 215 Little Collins Street. Phone: 63 0441. (Singles from $26 and doubles from $33, more for ones with private bathroom and television.)

Spencer Hotel and Motel, 44 Spencer Street. Phone: 62 6991. (Singles about $20, doubles about $30.)

Perth

Hostels

60-62 Newcastle Street. Phone: 325 5844. (Near city centre.)

46 Francis Street. Phone: 328 7794. (Both offer dorm beds for under $10.)

Private Hostels

Travel Mates, 496 Newcastle Street. Phone: 328 6685.

Top Notch Hostel, 194 Aberdeen Street. Phone: 328 6667. (Charges similar to YHA hostels.)

YMCA, 119 Murray Street. Phone: 325 2744 (very central. Rooms are about $10.)

YMCA Jewell House, 180 Goderich Street. Phone: 325 6973. (Singles are about $16, doubles $20, with long-term rates and kitchen facilities.)

Hotels

City Waters Lodge, 118 Terrace Road. Phone: 325 5020. (Rooms range around $30, central and near the lovely Swan River.)

Brittania Private Hotel, 253 William Street. Phone: 328 6121.

Brisbane

Hostels

Youth Hostel Association, 462 Queen Street and eight kilometres out at 15 Mitchell Street, Kedron. Phone: 571245.

Hotels

Budget Yale Inn, 413 Upper Edward Street. Phone: 832 1665 (with breakfast, singles are $18 and doubles are $24.)

Dorchester Holiday Flats, 484 Upper Edward Street, Phone: 831 2967.

Adelaide
Hostels
Youth Hostel, 290 Gilles Street. Phone: 223 6007

Private Hostels
Adelaide Backpackers Hostel, 263 Gilles Street. Phone: 223 5680. (Under $10 for a dorm bed.)
YMCA, Flinders Street. Phone: 223 1611 (Takes guests of either sex, central and comfortable with a cheap cafeteria. Dorms, singles and doubles, with weekly rates.)

Hotels
Afton Private Hotel, 260 South Terrace. Phone: 223 3416.
The Metropolitan Hotel, 46 Grote Street. Phone: 515 471. (Both central and cheap, with a room for about $14.)

Darwin
Hostels
Darwin Youth Hostel, Beaton Road, Hidden Valley Road, Berrimah. Phone: 84 3107. (Unfortunately twelve kilometres from the city centre, otherwise good, with dorm beds under ten dollars, bike hire and cheap trips organised by the hostel.)

Private Hostels
YMCA, Doctor's Gully end of the Esplanade. Phone: 81 8377. (Takes women and men, near city centre, dorms and rooms.)
YWCA, 119 Mitchell Street. Phone: 81 8644. (Takes men and women and does breakfast.)
Lameroo Lodge, 69 Mitchell Street. Phone: 81 9733. (Wide range of dorms, rooms and rooms with facilities.)

Irish Representatives

The Irish Embassy	Irish Consulate
20 Arkana Street,	10 Lilika Road,
Yarralumla,	City Beach,
ACT 2600.	WA 6015
Phone: 733 022	Phone: 272 8888

Major CES offices

Brisbane: Block B, Adelaide Street, Brisbane, Qld. 4000.
Darwin: Palmeston Building, Cavenach and Knuckey Street, Darwin, Northern Territory.

Perth: City Centre Tower, 44 St Georges Terrace, Perth, WA 6000.
Adelaide: 45 Grenfell Street, Adelaide, SA 5000.
Melbourne: 367 Collins Street, Melbourne, Vic 3000.
Sydney: 818 George Street, Railway Square, Broadway, Sydney, NSW 2000.

Irish Clubs and Associations

NSW
Irish National Association Australasia, 64 Devonshire Street, Surry Hills, Sydney, NSW 2010.
The Aisling Society, 21 Canterbury Road, Canterbury, NSW 2193.
NSW GAA, 13 Warrwillah Road, Five Dock, NSW 2046.
Penrith Gaels, PO Box 769, Penrith, NSW 2750.
Irish Australian Club, PO Box 11, Woonona, NSW 2516.
Kerrymans Association of NSW, 13 Warwillah Road, Five Dock, NSW 2046.

Victoria
The Celtic Club, 320 Queen Street, Melbourne, Vic 3000.
Irish National Day Council, 17 Maher Street, Fawkner, Vic 3060.
GAA of Victoria, 11 Edgeware Close, Kealba, Vic 3021.
Australian Irish Welfare Bureau, 155 Brunswick Street, Fitzroy, Vic 3065.
Latrobe Valley Irish Australian Cultural Association, ANZ bank, PO Box 554, Traralgon, Vic 3844.

South Australia
Irish Australian Association, Irish Memorial Hall, 11-15 Carrinton Street, Adelaide, SA 5000.
GAA, 81 Midway Road, Elizabeth, SA 5112.
Adelaide Irish Pipe Band, 45 Winchester Street, St Peters, SA 5069.
Australian Irish Dancing Association, 9 Tamar Crescent, Banksia Park, SA 5091.

Queensland
Queensland Irish Association, Tara House, 175 Elizabeth Street, Brisbane, Qld 4000.
Queensland GAA, 157 Birdwood Terrace, Toowong, Qld

4068.
North Queensland Irish Association, PO Box 248, Mount Isa,
Qld 4825.

Western Australia
GAA, PO Box 245, Subiaco, WA 6008.
The Irish Club of WA, PO Box 560, West Perth, WA 6005.
Shamrock Social Club, 16 Letson Bay, Langford, WA 6155.
WA Irish Pipe Band, 95 Jean Street, Hamilton Hill, WA 6163.

Northern Territory
Irish Association, Gaden Circuit, Jingilli, Darwin, NT.

Australian Capital Territory
Canberra Irish Club, PO Box 160, Belconnen, ACT 2616.

Advice on emigration

Emigrant Advice (under the auspices of the Dublin Diocesan
Social Service Centre), 1A Cathedral Street,
Dublin 1.
Phone: 732844.

Manpower,
O'Connell Bridge House,
Dublin 2.
Phone: 711544.

Information and advice on airfares

DLS Travel,
37 College Green,
Dublin 2.
Phone: 793991.

Australian Banks in London

Commonwealth Bank, 1 Kingsway, London WC2B 6DV.
Phone: 379 0955.
Westpac, Walbrook House, 23 Walbrook, London EC4N
4RA.
Phone: 626 4500.
State Bank of Victoria, Melbourne House, 48 Aldwych, London WC2B.
Phone: 379 7966.

State Bank of South Australia, 29 Pall Mall, London SW1Y 5LR.
Phone: 489 0300.
Rural & Industries Bank of Western Australia, 7th floor, Granite House, 97-101 Cannon Street, London EC4N 5AJ.
Phone: 623 7722.

National Trust

ACT: 42 Franklin Street, Manuka 2603.
NSW: Observatory Hill, Sydney 2000, NSW
NT: 14 Knuckey Street, Darwin 5790 (GPO Box 3520) NT.
Queensland: Old Government House, George Street, Brisbane 4000, (GPO Box 1494), Qld.
South Australia: Ayers House, 288 North Terrace, Adelaide 5000, SA.
Tasmania: 25 Kirkway Place, Hobart 7000, Tas.
Victoria: Tasma Terrace, Parliament Place, Melbourne 3002, Vic.
WA: Old Perth Boys School, 139 St Georges Terrace, Perth 6000.

National Park Organisations

NSW: National Parks & Wildlife Service, 189-193 Kent Street, Sydney 2000.
Northern Territory: National Parks & Wildlife Service, 1st Floor, Commercial Union Building, Smith Street, Darwin 5794.
Queensland: National Parks & Wildlife Service, 239 George Street, Brisbane 4000.
South Australia: National Parks & Wildlife Service, 129 Greenhill Road, Unley 5061.
Tasmania: National Parks & Wildlife Service, 16 Magnet Court, Sandy Bay 7005.
Victoria: National Parks Service, 240 Victoria Parade, East Melbourne 3002.
Western Australia: National Parks Authority, Hackett Drive, Crawley 6009.
Australian Capital Territory: National Parks & Wildlife Service, 3rd Floor, Construction House, 217 Northbourne Avenue, Turner 2601.

Tourist Offices

Outside Australia
Australian Tourist Commission
Australian Tourist Commision,
4th Floor,
Heathcote House,
20 Saville Row,
London WIX 1AC,
England.
Phone: 434 4371
Publishes two useful booklets, *Campus Accommodation* (listing college accommodation possibilities) and *Down Under Wonder* (an introduction to geography, flora and fauna).

In Australia
Australian Capital Territory Government Tourist Bureau
City offices: Canberra, Melbourne, Sydney.
Head office: ACT Government Tourist Bureau,
Jolimont Centre,
Northbourne Avenue,
Canberra 2601,
ACT.
Phone: (062) 49 7555

West Australian Government Travel Centres (Holiday WA)
City offices: Perth, Melbourne, Sydney, Brisbane, Adelaide.
Head office: Holiday WA,
772 Hay Street,
Perth 6000,
WA.
Phone: (09) 322 2999

Victorian Government Travel Centres
City offices: Melbourne, Sydney, Canberra, Brisbane, Adelaide, Perth, Hobart.
Head office: Victorian Government Travel Centre,
230 Collins Street,
Melbourne 3000
Vic.
Phone: (03) 602 9444

Tasmanian Government Tourist Bureau (Tasbureau)
City offices: Hobart, Melbourne, Sydney, Brisbane, Adelaide, Perth, Canberra.
Head office: Tasbureau,
            80 Elizabeth Street,
            Hobart 7000,
            Tas.
            Phone: (002) 34 6911

Queensland Government Travel Centres
City offices: Brisbane, Sydney, Canberra, Melbourne, Adelaide, Perth.
Head office: Queensland Government Travel Centre,
            Corner Adelaide & Edward Streets,
            Brisbane 4000,
            Qld.
            Phone: (07) 31 2211

South Australian Government Travel Centres
City offices: Adelaide, Melbourne, Sydney.
Head office: South Australian Government Travel Centre,
            18 King William Street,
            Adelaide 5000,
            SA.
            Phone: (08): 212 1644

Travel Centres of New South Wales
City offices: Sydney, Brisbane, Melbourne, Adelaide.
Head office: NSW Government Travel Centre,
            16 Spring Street (corner Pitt & Spring),
            Sydney 2000.
            Phone: (02) 231 4444

Northern Territory Government Tourist Bureau
City offices: Darwin, Melbourne, Sydney, Perth, Hobart, Brisbane, Adelaide, Canberra.
Head office: Northern Territory Government Tourist
            Bureau,
            27 Smith Street,
            Darwin 5750,
            NT.
            Phone: (089) 81 6611

Customs Inquiries

You should direct any inquiries to the Collector of Customs at the port where you will import the goods. The addresses are:

The Collector of Customs
Sydney, New South Wales 2000
Phone: (02) 226 5000
Telex: 73909

The Collector of Customs
Melbourne, Victoria 3000
Phone: (03) 611 1555
Telex: 30956

The Collector of Customs
Brisbane, Queensland 4000
Phone: (07) 835 0444
Telex: 40183

The Collector of Customs
Port Adelaide, South Australia 5015
Phone: (08) 479211
Telex: 82155

The Collector of Customs
Fremantle, Western Australia 6000
Phone: (09) 430 1444
Telex: 92744

The Collector of Customs
Hobart, Tasmania 7000
Phone: (002) 30 1201
Telex: 58009

The Collector of Customs
Darwin, Northern Territory 5790
Phone: (089) 81 4444
Telex: 85043

The Comptroller-General
Australian Customs Service
Canberra, ACT 2600
Phone: (062) 72 3922
Telex: 62049

Quarantine Inquiries: General

The Australian Quarantine Service,
Department of Health,
PO Box 100,
Woden,
Canberra,
ACT 2606.

Dog and Cat Importation:
Assistant Director-General,
Animal Quarantine,
Department of Health,
GPO Box 100
Woden
ACT 2606.

Wildlife and Wildlife products, protected species:
    The Director,
    Australian National Parks and Wildlife Service,
    GPO Box 636,
    Canberra,
    ACT 2601.

Customs Inquiries: Business
    Department of Industry and Commerce,
    Barton,
    Canberra,
    ACT 2600

14 Books About Australia

Tide Directory, Youth Emigration Action Group, 1987, £10.
This collection of photostats is an introduction to emigration to twelve countries, so space for each one is very limited. Australia gets only eight pages.

Amhráin ó Dheireadh an Domhain, le Fionán Mac Cártha, Oifig an tSoláthair, 1953.
This little book contains 35 poems by Fionán Mac Cártha, the man Dúbhglás de hÍde described as 'the best Connaught poet since Raftery'. In a poignant foreword, addressed from Amby, Queensland, Mac Cártha laments 'níl Gaedhilgeoir i bhfoiseacht míle míle dhom annso, agus ní mór an méid leabhar Gaedhilge atá agam acht oiread.'

The Australian Almanac, Angus & Robertson, 1986, $16 (approx), 800 pp.
This paperback book, on cheap paper, puts the emphasis on what is available rather than what is needed in the way of information. Fairly well organised, it can serve as a background reference book on many areas of Australian life. It also includes a great deal of international information.

Australia Handbook, Australian Government Publishing Service, 1986, free, 160 pp.
This paperback book is pocket-sized, expensively produced on glossy paper, and has colour photographs. It is a good introduction to Australia, but gives more of a general run-down on each area than specific facts, figures and dates.

The Concise Australian Reference Book, Golden Press, 1986, $16, 504 pp.
This neat hardback is packed with useful information about Australia, including much that you will never need unless you are world champion class in Trivial Pursuit. It is well-organised and the information is grouped into logical areas of interest.

Australian Jobs Directory, 1987, £8.50.
This is mainly a selection from the Australian Yellow Pages, company names and addresses grouped in business categories.There are also small information sections, many of them reprints of Australian Government handouts. Look

out for mistakes. Large format (A4), 80 pages, printed on one side.

Long Stays in Australia, by Maggie Driver, David & Charles, £11.44, 190 pp.
This hardback book is written in a chatty style, short on facts (and not all of those correct). It nods towards the Irish, but is aimed mainly at English people thinking of spending some time in Australia. One in a series of 'long stays' books.

Australia – a travel survival kit, by Tony Wheeler, Lonely Planet, 1986, £11.44, 616 pp.
This is the best guide book for those going touring in Australia. Lonely Planet, probably the best guide-book publishers for the budget traveller, started out in Australia. This bulky paperback crams in at least a few lines about just about everywhere, plus travel and accommodation information. There is not much on work, visas, history or the social system, but it is a must for the holidays.

The Insider's Guide to Australia, by Robert Wilson, Merehurst Press, 1987, £10.29, 220 pp.
This paperback tourist guide has a city-by-city run-down on Australia, illustrated with photographs and maps. It has plenty on where to go, how to get there and what so see but, although good, it is still not as good as Lonely Planet.

MORE MERCIER BESTSELLERS

Botany Bay

The story of the convicts transported
from Ireland to Australia, 1791 - 1853

Con Costello

Between 1791 and 1853 about 45,000 Irish convicts – men and women – were transported to Australia. The majority of the transportees went in the 212 convict ships which sailed from Dublin or the Cove of Cork. The others were included in the convict fleets from England.

Until comparatively recent years a convict in one's ancestry was an embarrassment in Australia. Now, when the realities of the offences of those transported have been researched and analysed, a better understanding of the character of these people can be found.

In *Botany Bay* Con Costello has investigated the social background of the period, the procedures under which the accused persons were tried, imprisoned and transported. A grim picture of life in the prisons, hulks and convict ships emerges. On arrival in Australia the bewildered transportees faced further hardship and prejudice. But it is not all a story of depression and degradation. The bulk of the men and women found a tolerable life in the new land. A good number of them became prosperous and encouraged their families to join them in Australia. The Irish contribution to the making of Australia is well acknowledged.

IRISH BALLADS AND SONGS OF THE SEA
Compiled by James N. Healy

Our ballads of the sea have a wonderful variety about them, if only for the reason that 'the sea carried our manhood to die in Spain, to fight in France, to be transported to Van Diemen's Land; and following the dreadful days of a famine in the middle of the last century, to become rich in the Golden Land of Americay'.

BALLADS FROM THE PUBS OF IRELAND
Compiled by James N. Healy

A thoroughly enjoyable, roistering collection of sad songs, merry lyrics and ballads of love that people roar out with a depth of feeling in the pubs of Ireland.

THE SONGS OF PERCY FRENCH
James N. Healy

The well-loved songs in this volume are the airs you heard whistled on the street or sung in your favourite pub, including among others, 'The Mountains of Mourne', 'Phil the Fluther's Ball', 'Come Back Paddy Reilly', 'Are Ye Right There, Michael', 'The Darling Girl from Clare' and 'Shlatherty's Mounted Fut'. Percy French, Ireland's leading troubadour, was without doubt the most prolific of Irish song writers.

SONGS OF STRUGGLE AND PROTEST
Edited by John McDonnell

The words and music of 45 songs, each placed in its historical and social context including 'The Red Flag', 'Joe Hill', 'The Times They Are A Changing' and 'The Men Behind the Wire'.

THE IRISH WOMAN'S SONGBOOK
Carmel O Boyle

The Irish Woman's Songbook is a selection of 50 songs, six of which are in Irish and the rest are in English, including 'The Bunch of Thyme', 'Dónal Og', 'The High Hills of Derry' and 'The Suit of Green'. They are intended to be sung by women, particularly Irish women.

LOVE SONGS OF THE IRISH
James N. Healy

A collection of Ireland's best-loved traditional love songs ranging from the early seventeenth century to the present day – from Carolan to Thomas Moore to the contemporary John B. Keane.

O'NEILL'S IRISH MUSIC
400 CHOICE SELECTIONS FOR PIANO OR VIOLIN
Captain Francis O'Neill

Here are no less than 400 of the very best of Irish airs, jigs, reels, hornpipes, etc. from O'Neill's celebrated collection. Suitable for piano, violin and most other instruments. This collection will provide musicians with hours of joy in playing these wonderful old tunes. This is a reprint of the original and enlarged edition first published in 1915 in Chicago.

IRISH MINSTRELS AND MUSICIANS
The story of Traditional Irish Music, its Collectors and Performers
Captain Francis O'Neill

Originally published in 1913, this book affords a fascinating insight into the world of Irish music through its wide-ranging contents. The book is crammed with historical research, valuable information on techniques, and many articles on individual ace performers of the past. Born near Bantry, Co. Cork, O'Neill went on to become Chief of Chicago's police force, where he commenced on his task of collecting music from many of the emigrant arrivals. A complete biography of O'Neill by Brendan Breathnach completes this richly illustrated book.

even demonstrate some leadership. Thus self-esteem begins to improve.

Discarding is initially a process of perception. People come to see that the change is both inevitable and/or necessary. Adaptation starts with recognition. Here we see human courage in difficult circumstances as the individual accepts new 'realities'. This can be exciting for individuals and groups. In taking the risk of publicly facing a new reality, there is a sense in which they reestablish their own identity; the identity which may have seemed threatened by the changes being introduced.

The crisis of change creates great tensions within the people involved. These provide many reasons for people to feel upset and disorientated: a new job appears to be of lesser status than the old one; valued skills seem unnecesary; the new work seems frustrating; the new system appears to be unusual, even frightening, although with practice it becomes commonplace. The crucial point is that this process needs time. Discarding involves experimentation and risk. Time is needed for individuals to recreate their own sense of identity and self-esteem as they 'grow' into the new situation.

Stage 4: adaptation

Now a process of mutual adaptation emerges. Rarely do new systems, procedures, structures or machines work effectively first time. Individuals begin to test the new situation and themselves, trying out new behaviours, working to different standards, working out ways of coping with the changes. Thus the individual learns. Other individuals also adapt. Fellow workers, supervisors and managers all learn as the new system is tried out. Finally, technical and operational problems are identified and modifications made to solve them. Thus progress is made.

Significant amounts of energy are involved during this stage. Often the process of trial and error, of effort and setback, and the slow building of performance can be a source of real frustration. In these circumstances people can appear angry. This is not resistance to change, rather it is the natural consequence of trying to make a new system work, experiencing partial or complete failure, which may or may not be under the control of the individuals concerned. This anger is not evidence of attempts to oppose but rather it articulates the feelings of those trying to make the new system work. Whilst managers should ensure the right training and support is available, they should generally remain in the background, allowing the people directly involved to make the new system work. By doing so these people will develop the skills, understanding and attachments needed for the system to be run effectively in the longer term.

Stage 5: internalization

The people involved have created a new system, process and organization. New relationships between people and processes have been tried, modified and accepted. These have become incorporated into the understanding of the new work situation. This is a cognitive process through which people make sense of what has happened. Now the new behaviour becomes part of 'normal' behaviour.

It seems that people experience change in these ways, initially as disturbance, perhaps even as a shock, then come to accept its reality, testing it out and engaging in a process of mutual adaptation and finally, they come to terms with it. Self-esteem and performance vary, during the process initially declining, and then growing again. The variation in performance flows from mutually reinforcing individual and operational causes, as has been observed. The 'engine' for rebuilding performance is the self-esteem of the people involved.

It is not suggested that people go through these stages neatly, nor that all go through them at the same time, or at the same rate. Some may not go beyond the denial of change. The important point is that people do seem to experience significant changes in these ways and this leads us to a number of practical ways in which the problems of coping can be handled. Coping with the process of change places demands on the individuals involved. Various issues need to be faced either by the individuals or by managers. Note, however, that these issues are of concern to all affected by an organizational change, including managers.

REBUILDING SELF-ESTEEM

The ground covered in this section is summarized in Figure 8.4. In simple terms, it is suggested that individuals have four main categories of need which are required if they are to rebuild their

Figure 8.4 Rebuilding self-esteem

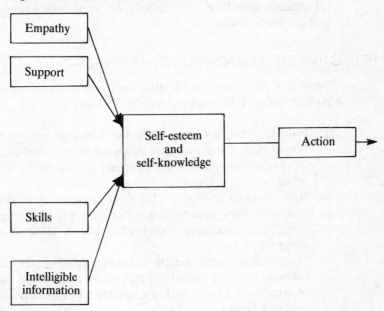

self-esteem during a programme of organizational change. They need intelligible information. They will probably need to develop new skills, even if only the skill of dealing with new people as colleagues or supervisors. They will need support to help them deal with the problems and encouragement to try out new systems. Provision of short workshops planned to achieve part or all of the work discussed in the preceding section can help. Technical support to solve problems is often needed. Access to people who can help is useful. Control over the rate of personal learning should be possible. All of these things can help, but most of all people need to be treated with empathy. First and foremost empathy is the main factor.

Understanding is a key issue. The skill of empathy is the struggle to understand. People can never fully see a situation as others see it but they can struggle to try, and individuals will respond to that struggle. They will also respond adversely to someone who clearly does not try. Making information intelligible to its recipient requires skill. People need to try to see things as the recipient will, in order to communicate, but if they pass on the information they have, they usually do so without attempting to make it intelligible.

EFFECTIVE IMPLEMENTATION OF CHANGE

Some guidelines for the effective implementation of change can now be outlined. Managing change requires us to:

1 Provide people with help to deal with change, recognizing the valued skills that they may now no longer use, and encourage them to see the future benefits of change, where this is appropriate.
2 Avoid over-organizing so that there is flexibility to deal with problems. New systems are never 100 per cent successful straightaway. Managers need the flexibility to allow adaptation along the way.
3 Communicate, communicate, always communicate! Effective communication is crucial but this means quality, not quantity, of communication. Check the quality of communication via feedback from staff.
4 Recognize that the problems others experience are real problems. Empathize. Don't ignore them, face up to them.
5 Gain full commitment to change by supporting people. Reward them, provide positive feedback and involve them at an early stage.

All of this requires a more systematic and sensitive approach to how change is planned and managed, an approach that is sensitive to the needs of people and sensitive to the problems and opportunities of the business. We hope this book has provided you with some techniques to help you approach change management in this way.

REFERENCES

Adams, J., Hayes, J. and Hopson, B (1976) *Transitions – Understanding and Managing Personal Change,* Oxford: Martin Robertson.